THE MYSTERY OF THE TAROT

The origins of the Tarot are so veiled in the mists of time that it is only natural for myths and legends to surround it. Superstition, flights of fancy, and speculation have added their own patterns to the rich and colorful tapestry of Tarot lore and have only deepened its aura of magic and mystery. Cults have grown up around one or another historical theory, and sometimes their adherents have become fanatical in proclaiming the one and only "truth." But the better-informed investigators retain a certain amount of flexibility—even skepticism—and make no ironclad assertions.

The truest claim we can make is that the Tarot is a symbolic record of human experience. Through deeply rooted mystic powers, the cards accomplish miracles of psychological insight, wise counsel and accurate divination.

A COMPLETE GUIDE TO THE
TAROT

BY EDEN GRAY

BANTAM BOOKS
TORONTO · NEW YORK · LONDON

A NATIONAL GENERAL COMPANY

A COMPLETE GUIDE TO THE TAROT

*A Bantam Book / published by arrangement with
Crown Publishers, Inc.*

PRINTING HISTORY
Crown edition published June 1970
2nd printing . . . October 1970
3rd printing . . . February 1971
Universe Book Club January 1971 Selection
Bantam edition published June 1972
2nd printing
3rd printing

Published simultaneously in the United States and Canada

*Bantam Books are published by Bantam Books, Inc., a National
General company. Its trade-mark, consisting of the words "Bantam
Books" and the portrayal of a bantam, is registered in the United
States Patent Office and in other countries. Marca Registrada.
Bantam Books, Inc., 666 Fifth Avenue, New York, N.Y. 10019.*

PRINTED IN THE UNITED STATES OF AMERICA

CONTENTS

ACKNOWLEDGMENTS

My deep appreciation to Nan Braymer for her invaluable assistance in the preparation of the manuscript of this book.

Also to Mary Beckwith Cohen for her advice on all matters that concerned Astrology.

THE TAROT DEFINED

The ancient and mystic pack of cards called the Tarot never fails to evoke the curiosity of the uninitiated. "What are the Tarot cards?" "What makes them so different from our own playing cards?" "Can they really foretell the future?" "Can anyone learn how to read them?"

This book is devoted to answering these and many other questions and to give the reader a knowledge of the Tarot—its history, its links to other occult sciences, and the way it is used to shed light upon the past, the present, and the future.

Everyone agrees that modern playing cards are directly descended from one part of the Tarot—the resemblances between parent and child are too striking to be accidental. In both we find cards numbered one to ten, followed by pictures or "court" cards. And just as the Joker is unnumbered and has no assigned place in our deck, the Fool in the Tarot is also without a number of its own or a pre-ordained position—yet both are ever present in their respective packs.

There are 78 cards in the Tarot, of which 56 (those most like modern cards) are equally divided among four suits—Wands, Cups, Swords, Pentacles—analogous to our Clubs, Hearts, Spades, and Diamonds. These suit cards are known as the Minor Arcana (*arcana* is the Latin word for secrets). They are followed by 22 cards called the Major Arcana—cards that depict symbolic figures, elements in nature, the experiences of Man in his spiritual journey, his hopes and fears, his joys and sorrows.

The Major Arcana, as can be seen, bear little resemblance to modern cards. Their illustrations are drawn from the treasurehouse of universal symbols and images, from the legends, myths, philosophies, religions, and magic beliefs of the human race. Undoubtedly the wise men and seers through whom the Tarot is believed to have been transmitted over more than seven centuries were thoroughly versed in the astrological, numerological, and Kabalistic teachings of the ancients, and all these influences are reflected in the cards. The Tarot, nevertheless, remains a unique and independent discipline with its own divinatory powers and its own spiritual content.

Most of us are interested in character analysis, glimpses of the future, solutions to immediate dilemmas—all of which we can seek in the Tarot. But there are also those who will value the Tarot's help in meditation. The student of metaphysics gains remarkable insights into the inner meanings of the cards; the artist, constantly concerned with images and symbols, draws heightened creativity from contemplating the many-dimensional beauty of the cards; the Biblical student finds that the Tarot illuminates many passages in the Old and New Testaments. And since the Tarot is the key that unlocks the wisdom of the ancient philosophers, it reveals its most profound messages to the dedicated scholar and practitioner. (In this it is not unlike the ideographic writing of the Chinese, the hieroglyphics of the Egyptians, the picture writing of the Mayans.)

It is not necessary, however, to understand all the hidden secrets of the cards at first—or even second—glance. When the student is ready, the Tarot will begin to reveal its mysteries. And it is not imperative to "believe in the cards" for them to yield results—you don't have to take them on blind faith. Eventually you will tap the occult powers of the Tarot, and you will turn to it when dilemmas beset you.

If you consult an experienced "Reader" for help, you become what is called the "Querent," with an unspoken question you want answered. After laying out the cards in accordance with one of the methods described in this book, the Reader will interpret what the cards are trying to tell you. But you yourself can learn the definitions of the symbols as given in the Glossary, as well as from the detailed descriptions and pictures of each of the cards in the body of the book. Then, after mastering one or another of the techniques for laying the cards out, you can before long try to read them. At first, of course, you will be turning back to the definitions again and again, but with persistence you will be rewarded.

The first Tarot cards were painted on parchment or thin sheets of ivory, silver, or even gold. The design for each card had to be drawn anew and colored by hand. Therefore the cards became the playthings of the nobles, who could afford to assign an artist to paint their own individual sets. Often the aristocracy had the Court cards drawn to resemble members of their own family or court.

Eventually, handmade cardboard became available, and then the designs were traced and painted with watercolors. Later still, in Nuremberg (about 1430), block printing was done from hand-carved wooden blocks. Thus some of the early cards are crude in design, and their details are often indistinct.

To reduce the cost of a Tarot deck, or perhaps because the Major Arcana were not used in the game of Tarroc, these 21 cards were dropped from the pack, as were the four Queens. At a later date, the Queens were evidently restored to some decks, and the Knights eliminated. Decks in this latter form are to this day used in the Spanish and Italian game of Tarroc. The cards from southern Germany developed a somewhat different pattern—bells for Pentacles, acorns for Swords, leaves for Wands, and hearts for Cups.

The cards depicted in this book are only one set of the many that have appeared during the long history of the Tarot. They are those used by A. E. Waite in his book *The Pictorial Key to the Tarot* (1910), and they have become standard for most of the English-speaking world. First published by William Rider & Son, Ltd., they are called the Rider Pack.

When people ask you, "What is the Tarot?" you should know a good part of the answer after you have read the text and studied the strange and beautiful pictures. Those who are embarking on this quest for wisdom and guidance will find it an exciting and rewarding journey with the help of the Tarot—our priceless heritage from the ancients.

HISTORY OF THE TAROT

The true Tarot is symbolism: it speaks a language that arises from the collective mind of Man. Given an understanding of the inner meaning of the symbols, the cards yield, on the highest plane, mystic powers and esoteric wisdom. And although there are various theories about the Tarot and many different versions of the cards, no one of them can claim final truth and any one of them may contribute some illumination.

As an analogy, consider the hundreds of paintings and statues of Venus that have been made through the centuries. The goddess appears in numerous varied guises, according to the artist's own conceptions and the time in which he lived. Yet the representations retain recognizable characteristics, even though not only ideas but also styles and methods of drawing, painting, and sculpting are constantly changing.

So it has been with the Tarot. Occultists, historians, and artists have modified details as new researches present new evidence, but the best of these changes retain the basic symbolism.

The origins of the Tarot are so veiled in the mists of time that it is only natural for myths and legends to have grown up—particularly around the Major Arcana. Superstition, flights of fancy, and speculation have added their own patterns to the rich and colorful tapestry of Tarot lore and, curiously enough, have only deepened its aura of magic and mystery. Cults have grown up around one or another historical theory, and sometimes their adherents have become fanatical in proclaiming the one and only "truth." But the better-informed investigators retain a certain amount of flexibility—even skepticism—and make no ironclad assertions.

The Gypsies say that the hidden knowledge of the Tarot was originally brought by their people from Chaldea and Egypt into Israel and thence to Greece. "Papus" (Dr. Gerard Encausse), a leading French occultist, is quoted as saying: "The Gypsy . . . has given us the key which enables us to explain all the symbolism of the ages. . . . In it, where a man of the people sees only the key to an obscure tradition, [are] discovered the mysterious links which unite God, the Universe and Man."

It seems incontrovertible that there is some link between the Tarot and the Gypsies in their worldwide wanderings. The Gypsies did indeed roam through Europe at about the same time that the Tarot cards began to be used around the shores of the Mediterranean. They are heard of in Austria in the twelfth century and in Rumania in the fourteenth. (It is interesting to note that the Hungarian Gypsy's word for a pack of cards is "tar.")

Legend has it that as pagan cults became the victims of Christian persecution, the Hierophants (priests of the Eleusinian Mysteries) handed down their ancestral lore to the Gypsies, who undertook to transmit it only to those deemed worthy. For who would suspect that a wandering Gypsy was the custodian of so precious a treasure? It is said that the Gypsy was also entrusted with the secrets of the Gnostics, the Montanists, and the Manichaeans, as well as the Albigenses. These last were one of the sects of the Cathari, whose headquarters were the town of Albi. They flourished in the twelfth century but were exterminated in the thirteenth by the Crusades and the Inquisition. The Albigenses accepted the belief in dualism, renouncing marriage and eating no animal food. The Gypsies claim they also guarded the mysteries that were later embodied in the Jewish Kabalah, as well as those of the Masonic Order.

One of the most fascinating stories claiming that the Tarot originated in Egypt relates that after the great library at Alexandria was destroyed, the city of Fez (in what is now Morocco) became the intellectual capital of the world, to which wise men traveled from near and far. Needing to create a common tongue—for they spoke in many languages—they set about inventing a method of communication. To this end, they prepared a picture book abounding in mystic symbols. A key to the meanings of these signs was handed down by word of mouth from initiate to initiate. To preserve the secrecy of their messages, the symbols were later reproduced on seemingly innocuous cards that were used in games of chance by more frivolous men who could not possibly decipher their true significance.

Another hypothesis attributes the invention of the Tarot to Thoth, counselor to Osiris. He was the scribe of the Egyptian gods, measurer of time, inventor of numbers, and the god of wisdom and magic, who is often depicted as having the head of the ibis. It has also been reported that interpretations of the 22 cards of the Major Arcana at one time formed part of the initiation ceremonies for the Egyptian priesthood. One thing is certain: many of the Tarot symbols are clearly derived from Egyptian mythology.

A study of the cards also discloses a close relationship to the Kabalistic lore of the ancient Hebrews. In short, there can be no doubt that whoever actually invented the Tarot knew ancient religions and philosophies and embodied many of their symbols in the cards. However, their deeper implications may have been lost or deliberately hidden during the time when the Gypsies of southern France, Spain, and Italy used them as their stock-in-trade in telling fortunes.

Granting these influences (as well as those of the Hebrew alphabet, color symbolism, Numerology, and Astrology), the truest claim we can make is that the Tarot is a symbolic record of human experience. Through deeply rooted mystic powers, the cards accomplish miracles of psychological insight, wise counsel, and accurate divination.

The earliest date attributed to the Tarot cards seen in European museums is 1390, though the actual origin of the cards is said to go back to the twelfth century. In the Museo Correr at Venice, there are some cards dating from around 1445; the so-called Minchiati set, of about the same period, is thought to be in private hands in Milan.

In the fourteenth century, Jacques Gringonneur, astrologer and Kabalist, is said to have invented playing cards for the amusement of Charles VI of France. There is some doubt that these were complete Tarot decks, but one suspects that they may well have been part of a deck with astrological and Kabalistic symbols that Gringonneur had been working on for years.

In England, the Tarot was known in the reign of Edward IV (fifteenth century). The king forbade the importation of the cards; nevertheless, the Tarot found its way from the caravans of the Gypsies into the homes of the nobles, where it was kept hidden for fear of reprisals. After the French Revolution, a new freedom swept Europe; esoteric sects and mystic lodges flourished once again.

In the eighteenth century, the illustrious French scholar Court de Gébelin, who was the first to suggest that the Tarot might be of Egyptian origin, unearthed the Tarot cards while doing research for his many-volumed works. Gébelin's rediscovery came at a time when people were interested in Rosicrucianism, Masonry, the Kabalah, and Astrology. The climate was propitious for the Tarot and its mysticism to reenter the occult thought of the day. The "Marseilles deck," the cards frequently used as a source today, stem from those depicted in Gébelin's book *Le Monde Primitif*, published in 1773.

Ten years later, a fashionable fortuneteller named Ettiela undertook to restore to their original form Court de Gébelin's version of the Tarot figures. In doing this he added some highly unorthodox changes of his own, which later experts discarded. Ettiela was the first, however, to suggest a link between the Tarot and Astrology and the Kabalah.

After a long interval, in 1854 there was a revival of interest with the publication of Eliphas Levi's *Dogma and Ritual of Transcendental Magic*. This book, the first in a series of occult writings by Levi, names the Tarot as his prime source. He traces the connection between the 22 cards of the Tarot's Major Arcana and the 22 letters of the Hebrew alphabet. In his book, he places the Fool,

Key 0, between Keys 20 and 21, and this sequence has been followed by French occultists ever since.

The Hermetic Order of the Golden Dawn was founded in England in 1886 as a result of the discovery and deciphering of some ancient manuscripts on occult initiation. One of the interests of the members of the Order seems to have been the proper placing of the Fool in the pack. The leader of the Golden Dawn, S. L. MacGregor Mathers, author of *The Kabalah Unveiled*, later wrote a small booklet called *The Tarot, Its Occult Signification, Use in Fortune-Telling, and Method of Play, Etc.* This is again in print.

In 1889, "Papus" (Dr. Gerard Encausse) published *The Tarot of the Bohemians*, using revised designs by a contemporary, Oswald Wirth, and attributing Levi's interpretations to them. A. E. Waite wrote the preface to Papus's book when it was republished in England about 1900; that book is also now available.

Of all the old sets of cards that had sprung up through the centuries, some containing as many as 140 cards, it was generally agreed among occultists that the set known as the Marseilles Tarot was the purest source. It had the correct number of 22 Major Trumps, and the designs had suffered less corruption and distortion in the course of time.

Another member of the Golden Dawn, Arthur Edward Waite, an English occultist to whom we have referred more than once in these pages, published his own book, *The Pictorial Key to the Tarot*, in 1910. At his direction a new set of cards (the pack used in this book) was drawn by the well-known English artist Pamela Colman Smith, after Waite's own conception of the symbolism of the cards. This was called the Rider Pack. Waite was able to restore in great part the original symbolic meanings that had been lost or changed in the passage of time. There are those who say that the symbols had been deliberately changed, in some cases to throw the Roman Church off the track and prevent the priests from appropriating the Tarot's verities for their own purposes.

Paul Foster Case, an American, has published an excellent book, *The Tarot, A Key to the Wisdom of the Ages*. He was one of the last members of the Golden Dawn, and had access to their records and notes. Case presents only the Major Arcana, and uses some of the modifications of the Rider Pack; as I understand it, these are similar to the unpublished ones of the Golden Dawn.

A new English writer, Gareth Knight, exhibits great understanding of the Tarot in his two-volume work *A Practical Guide to Qabalistic Symbolism* (1965).

The exact placement of the Fool has always caused much discussion and still does; the English books on the subject have tried various placements in order to bring the meanings of the Hebrew alphabet more in line with the meanings of the cards. (This subject will be discussed more fully in the section on the Tarot and the Kabalah.) Aleister Crowley, controversial English critic and devotee of Black Magic, became a member of the Order of the Golden Dawn, as did Israel Regardie, for some years Crowley's secretary. Both felt that the Fool should be placed before Key 1 in the Major Arcana, since zero precedes the number one. Crowley, in *The Book of Thoth* (1944), says that this is obviously the proper place and that any mathematician would agree.

Many other contemporary scholars, writers, and psychologists have been interested in, and inspired by, the study of the Tarot. Psychoanalysts have looked with respect upon the symbols and their connection with the subconscious activities of the human psyche. Among those who have taken cognizance of the Tarot are T. S. Eliot, in *The Waste Land;* Charles Williams, in *The Greater Trumps;* William Lindsay Gresham, in *Nightmare Alley;* and P. D. Ouspensky, in *A New Model of the Universe.* A. E., the famous Irish poet, belonged to the Order of the Golden Dawn, and the poet W. B. Yeats was also a member of a secret order that dealt with the Tarot's occult traditions. The followers of the famous psychoanalyst C. G. Jung see symbols in the cards that relate to the archetypes of the collective unconscious. Albert Pike's *Morals and the Dogma of the Scottish Rites* makes reference to the cards; and Thomas Troward, a founder of New Thought and one of the clearest exponents of the Science of Mind, has devoted serious thought to the spiritual significance of this "oldest book known to man."

Thus, even though the precise time and place of the Tarot's genesis are not firmly established, and even though the Tarot has gone through many transmutations over the centuries (and the legends and myths still multiply), it survives serenely, elusive at times but inspiring, a living demonstration of the truth "that there are more things in heaven and earth . . . than are dreamt of" in most people's philosophies.

THE MAJOR ARCANA

The Major Arcana is comprised of 22 cards, ranging from Key 0, the Fool, to Key 21, the World. The illustrations are rich in symbolic and mythological figures, animals, natural phenomena and objects. The very names of the cards are suggestive of magic and mystery: The Wheel of Fortune, The Hierophant, The Hanged Man, for example. Unlike the Minor Arcana, they bear no relationship to modern playing cards.

The Major Arcana are, in all probability, linked with the mystical wisdom of the Greek god Hermes Trismegistus, identified with the Egyptian Thoth and supposed author of many writings on man's relationship to the world of the Spirit. Hermetic ideas reappear in the Kabalah, alchemy, magic, and Astrology, and their concentration on symbols can be regarded as a kind of private language for metaphysical and arcane concepts too subtle and elusive for words.

Symbolic keys, like material ones, are expected to fit locks and open doors. Systems like the Kabalah or the Tarot, however, do not accomplish this in a simple or direct manner. Here we find keys that fit more than one lock and locks that can receive more than one key. The correspondence between the 22 Major Arcana Keys and the 22 paths on the Tree of Life and the 22 letters of the Hebrew alphabet, as well as astrological signs, evokes complex and subtle associations that can never be rigidly confined. Here there is no "final authority"—everything that is part of the living stream moves and changes, and the Tarot is indeed in this category.

It may be helpful to think of the Tarot as representing the spokes of a huge wheel upon which each of us travels during his life on earth, experiencing materials and spiritual ups and downs. These are reflected in the cards when they are laid out by a Reader—their positions, juxtapositions, and combinations are all significant. The Fool, representing the Life-force before it comes into manifestation on the earth plane, is in the center of the wheel, moves to its outer edge through 21 phases of experience, and then returns to the center whence it came.

Thus, the designs illuminate the life of man, his joys and sorrows, his hopes and fears. Each of the Major Arcana represents a distinct principle, law, power, or element in Nature. These are drawn from a repository of symbols and images common to all men in all ages, from what has been called the "collective unconscious." They appear in our dreams, in the poet's flights of imagination, in the inspired work of artists, in the visions of saints and prophets; indeed, thinking in pictures is the universal heritage of man.

Many of these picture-symbols are defined in the Glossary of Symbolic Terms at the end of the book. When the meaning of the Minor and Major Arcana has been grasped, the additional information in the specimen layouts, the readings, and the Glossary should carry the reader well on the way to understanding some of the hidden wisdom of the Tarot. Personal experiences will take on deeper meanings as they are seen in the light of universal experience; the basic truths in other metaphysical realms—Astrology, Numerology, Religious Science—will also be illuminated.

When one reads the Tarot cards frequently, it is difficult not to become convinced that some power is present that directs their distribution. An extraphysical power (now studied in our universities as "psychokinetic effect") affects the unconscious movements of the person shuffling, cutting, and laying out the cards, and when they are dealt they seem to fall into positions that inevitably relate to the subject of the reading.

A word about Key 0, the Fool. Actually, it stands more or less alone, and there is no concrete evidence that it should be positioned as the first card of the Major Arcana. It is both before and after the 21 Keys—the sum total of all.

The Major Arcana

KEY 0
THE FOOL

Here we have a youth about to step off the edge of a precipice. He symbolizes the Lifepower before it enters into manifestation. Therefore he represents inexperience—which certainly can be foolish. He faces northwest, the direction of the unknown. The sun behind him is still rising, for the spiritual sun never reaches its zenith; if it did, it would descend and decrease in power. The wand over the youth's shoulder is a symbol of the will, and tied to it is a wallet that is thought to carry universal memory and instinct. (Another possible interpretation is that the wallet carries the four magic symbols that he will have to learn to use.)

The sign of the eagle on the wallet betokens virile strength and is also associated with the zodiacal sign Scorpio. The youth also carries a white rose, indicating that he is still free from animal forms of desire. The little white dog at the young man's heels has many possible meanings: he has been evolved from the wolf, showing that lower forms of life can be elevated and improved by human companionship; he also shows us that Nature is glad to follow along in Man's wake. The snowy mountains in several cards indicate the cold, abstract principles of mathematics, which govern all earthly phenomena.

The Fool is about to pass into the cycle of life through which each soul must journey—stages so graphically described in Bunyan's *Pilgrim's Progress*. Think of the youth as Spirit facing unknown possibilities of self-expression as he enters the world, an ignorant babe. He stands on spiritual heights, about to step down into manifestation.

Every man must journey forward and choose between good and evil. If he has no philosophy, he is the Fool.

Divinatory Meaning: The subject of the reading is a dreamer, a mystic. He has the desire to accomplish a great goal. He must be careful to make the right choice. If he thinks that "when ignorance is bliss, 'tis folly to be wise," then he is indeed the Fool.

THE FOOL.

Reversed: Folly, indiscretion, thoughtless action. The choice is likely to be faulty.

KEY 1
THE MAGICIAN

The Magician stands before a table on which are laid a Wand, a Cup, a Sword, and a Pentacle, representing the Minor Arcana and meaning Air, Fire, Water, and Earth. He is about to draw power from above to materialize his desires. Over his head is the cosmic lemniscate, shaped like a figure 8 on its side—a symbol of eternal life and dominion, indicating the harmonious interaction of the conscious and subconscious, idea and feeling, desire and emotion.

About the Magician's waist we see the well-known symbol of eternity—a serpent devouring its tail. About his head is a rose vine with red roses, representing desire. In front of him are more red roses intertwined with the white lilies of abstract thought. His inner garment is the white of purity; his outer robe, the red of desire, activity, and passion.

The hand holding the magic wand is the ego-consciousness reaching up for power while the other hand points to earth, as if the Magician wills earth's forces to be subservient to him. Or, it might be said that with one hand he reaches up to take the hand of the Infinite for accomplishment in the higher realms, while he reaches down with the other to encourage the evolution of the lower kingdoms—thus uniting Spirit and matter in eternity.

The Magician represents Man's will in union with the Divine achieving the knowledge and power to bring desired things into manifestation through conscious self-awareness.

Divinatory Meaning: Will, mastery, organizational skills, creative talents. The ability to take the power from above and direct it through desire into manifestation.

Reversed: Indecision, weak will, ineptitude. The use of power for destructive ends.

THE MAGICIAN.

KEY 2
THE HIGH PRIESTESS

The High Priestess is seated between two pillars from the Temple of Solomon—the black pillar of Boaz representing the negative life force, and the white one, Jachin, the positive life force.

Thomas Troward, in his book *The Hidden Power*, has this to say about the two pillars before the temple: "They contain the key to the entire Bible and to the whole order of Nature, and as emblems of the two great principles that are the pillars of the universe, they fitly stood at the threshold of that temple which was designed to symbolise all the mysteries of Being...."

The High Priestess is protecting on her lap a scroll of esoteric wisdom inscribed with the word "Tora" (Divine Law), for it is not for all eyes to see. The solar cross on her breast, with arms of equal length, represents the balance of the positive and negative forces. (The upright is the positive, male element; the horizontal, the negative, female element.) The veil between the pillars is decorated with pomegranates (female) and palms (male)—symbols indicating that the subconscious is potentially reproductive. The edge of her gown, which balances the crescent moon at her feet, trails out of the picture, indicating the stream of consciousness, which flows into the background of Key 3, the Empress, and reappears in later cards.

The High Priestess is the virgin daughter of the moon, and wears on her head the symbol of a full moon, with a waxing and waning image of the moon on each side. She is the eternal feminine, sometimes called Isis or Artemis. She corresponds to all the virgin goddesses of the ancient world, even to Eve before her union with Adam. She is spiritual enlightenment, inner illumination. Whereas the Fool and the Magician represent only the potentiality, the will, to create, the High Priestess has the latent power to manifest. She is the link between the seen and the unseen.

Divinatory Meaning: Unrevealed future, hidden influences at work. Of special value for artists, poets, composers, mystics. When this card appears in a man's reading, it represents the perfect woman all men dream of; in a

woman's reading, it may indicate that she can find such virtues in herself or in a friend.

Reversed: Conceit, sensual enjoyment. Accepting surface knowledge.

KEY 3
THE EMPRESS

The Empress is the Earth Mother, here seated in a bloom-
ing garden. A field of ripe wheat lies before her, sacred to
the Egyptian goddess Isis; behind her is seen the stream of
consciousness flowing between cypress trees, sacred to Venus.
The heart-shaped shield is inscribed with the symbol of
Venus. The Empress' hair is bound with a wreath of
myrtle—again reminiscent of Venus, as are the seven pearls
around her neck. She wears a crown of twelve stars, each
with six points, denoting dominion over the macrocosm, as
does her scepter surmounted by a globe.

The High Priestess symbolizes the virgin state of the
cosmic subconscious, but the Empress typifies the produc-
tive, generative activities in the subconscious after it has
been impregnated by seed ideas from the self-conscious. The
subconscious has control over all the steps of development
in the material world; therefore the Empress represents
the multiplicator of images.

She is the Goddess of Love, Venus, the symbol of universal fecundity. As the High Priestess is Isis veiled, the
Empress is Isis unveiled.

Divinatory Meaning: Material wealth, marriage, fertility
for would-be parents, for farmers, or for people in the
creative arts. If its position is not in the best placement
in relation to other cards, it sometimes indicates luxury
or dissipation.

Reversed: Infertility, loss of material possessions, inac-
tion, frittering away of resources. Possibility of destruction
by war and famine. Poverty may disrupt home. Psychological problems may cause instability.

THE EMPRESS.

KEY 4
THE EMPEROR

The Emperor sits on his throne, commanding and stately. He is a solar figure, Martian in character—as testified by the rams' heads (emblems of Mars) that decorate his throne and appear on his left shoulder. In his right hand (the active, male side) he holds an Egyptian ankh (also called the Crux Ansata, Cross of Life). The ankh too is one of the symbols of Venus. In the Emperor's left hand (the passive, female side) is the globe of dominion, showing that only through the feminine power of love can he balance Spirit and matter and thus have the true power to rule. He is seated against a background of bare mountains.

His Key is No. 4, and this indicates all that is stable— four-square, broad-based, a foundation for the building of law and order. The number 4 also has this significance in Numerology. Four is the number of the elements: Air, Earth, Fire, and Water; there are four seasons in the year, four points to the compass, and four rivers in the garden of Eden. And there are four letters in the sacred name of God, IHVH, standing for Jehovah.

To recapitulate: Key 1, the Magician, is the active principle of life; Key 2, the High Priestess, the passive principle; Key 3, the Empress, is the "word made flesh and dwelling amongst us." The Emperor is the *active* Father force contrasted with the active Mother force through whom his characteristics are brought forth. He is the Magician *after* his union with the High Priestess has changed her into the Empress and made him the father of her offspring.

The Emperor stands for domination of the material world, for authority, paternity, and the regulation of life by law.

Note that flesh is not the enemy of the Spirit but its vehicle; Spirit is not the enemy of the flesh but its driving force.

Divinatory Meaning: Leadership, mental activity, domination. War-making power, authority, paternity. The fruits of toil, the results of action. Controlled and directed sexual drive.

THE EMPEROR.

Reversed: Loss of control. Serious injury in battle. Emotional immaturity and bondage to parents. Possibility of being defrauded of one's inheritance.

KEY 5
THE HIEROPHANT

Here again we have a figure seated between two pillars, repeating the theme of duality seen in the pillars behind the High Priestess. These are the pillars of the Tree of Life from the Kabalah, one representing Mercy and the other Severity. Or it might be said that the one on the right hand is law, and the left one liberty to obey or disobey. Both are necessary, for obedience through compulsion can never bring freedom—man must choose. The capitals of the pillars are decorated with mystic symbols of sexual union. The crossed keys at the feet of the Hierophant, one gold and one silver, are the solar and lunar currents of energy. The two tonsured priests kneeling before him wear palliums to symbolize the yoke of union. The garment of one is decorated by the white lilies of thought; that of the other shows the roses of desire.

This master of the sacred mysteries wears the triple crown of a Pope, the lower design of trefoils representing the lower material world, the middle one representing the formative world, and the top tier representing the creative world. The symbol of three is repeated in his staff, revealing the realms of spirit, soul, and body. The letter W at the very top is the Hebrew letter *Vav*, meaning nail, means of union, link. Here it is used to suggest the linking of man to God through the inner voice.

It is of some significance that the number 5 is that of the planet Mercury, ruler of intelligence; 5 is also the number of Man or humanity.

The Hierophant represents traditional, orthodox teaching considered suitable to the masses. He is the ruling power of external religion, whereas the High Priestess teaches only in secret and to initiates.

Divinatory Meaning: Preference for the outer forms of religion, the ritual, the creed, the ceremony. The importance of social approval; the need to conform to society.

Reversed: Openness to new ideas, unconventionality. The card of the inventor as well as of the hippie. Take care that you do not become superstitious.

THE HIEROPHANT

KEY 6
THE LOVERS

Here we find Raphael, angel of the air, personifying the superconscious pouring down cosmic benediction on the two figures below. The man in the picture represents the conscious mind in the earlier keys, the Magician and the Emperor, as well as the King standing in the chariot in Key 7. The woman is the subconscious mind, the High Priestess and the Empress; behind her is the tree of the knowledge of good and evil, bearing the fruits of the five senses. The serpent of sensation climbs up the tree, for temptation comes from the subconscious. Behind the man is a leafless tree bearing the trefoil flames of the 12 signs of the Zodiac, each divided into three decans.

The Key is profoundly metaphysical in its symbolism. As the man looks at the woman and she looks up at the angel, the truth conveyed is that the conscious mind cannot approach the superconscious unless it passes through the subconscious—a thought to consider in meditation. The lovers stand here in friendly harmony, with nothing to hide from each other, as the nudity of the figures indicates. A harmonious and successful life depends on the cooperation between the conscious and the subconscious.

The mountain in this Key indicates the fruitfulness of correct thought.

Key 6 is often symbolized by a man standing between two women. There is a cupid with a bow and arrow above them. The meanings for divinatory purposes are derived from this older symbolism.

Divinatory Meaning: Choice, temptation, attraction. The struggle between sacred and profane love. Harmony of the inner and outer aspects of life.

Reversed: Quarrels, infidelity, danger of a broken marriage. Need to stabilize the emotions. Possibility of a wrong choice.

THE LOVERS.

KEY 7
THE CHARIOT

This key signifies victory for the triumphant king who has conquered on all planes, particularly those of the mind, science, and growth. He wears a diadem with an eight-pointed star, here representing dominion. The chariot stands for the human personality, which can be a vehicle for the expression of the Self. The symbol on the front of the chariot shows the wings of inspiration, above the Hindu sign of the union of positive and negative forces. The two sphinxes are again the outer pillars of the Tree of Life, related in this instance to Nature and not Spirit. They may pull in different directions if the will of the charioteer does not control them. In the hands of the king is the wand of will, with which he must control the sphinxes. The canopy of stars over his head indicates that celestial influences hang over him and affect his victory. On his shoulders are lunar crescents.

If his powers of observation are faulty, superficial, or fearful, the resulting sequence of subconscious reactions is bound to be destructive.

Key 7 means rest and victory, self-discipline and stability. The conqueror may not yet have conquered himself. Here we find both will and knowledge, but there is more desire to attain than proven power for real attainment.

Some occultists divide the Tarot Keys into three groups of seven cards each. In this case the number 7 indicates that the Fool has reached an outer triumph and is ready to learn further lessons in the next seven cards.

Divinatory Meaning: Triumph, success, control over the forces of nature—thus triumph over ill health as well as money difficulties or enemies of any sort, including one's own lower animal passions. This is a card of those who achieve greatness. It may also indicate travel in comfort. Mental and physical powers should lead to fulfillment.

Reversed: Decadent desires, possibility of ill health, restlessness and desire for change, an unethical victory.

THE CHARIOT.

KEY 8
STRENGTH

A woman garlanded with flowers is either closing or opening a lion's mouth. Above her head is the cosmic lemniscate of Eternal Life, indicating that she is in control, thanks to the spiritual power above her.

She is exhibiting spiritual courage and the power that emanates from it, for the lion represents the passions and lower nature of Man. For a consciousness aware of the sign of Eternity above it, there are no obstacles, nor can there be any fear of resistance.

Her simple white robe indicates purity. Around her waist there is a chain of roses—symbol of the union of desires, which creates such strength that wild, unconscious forces bow before it.

The message transmitted by this Key is that we must learn to create a balance between our spiritual and carnal natures and thus influence the lower of the two. This lesson of the need for harmony between opposing forces is often noted in the Tarot.

Divinatory Meaning: Force of character, spiritual power overcoming material power, love triumphing over hate, the higher nature over carnal desires.

Reversed: Domination of the material. Discord, lack of moral force, fear of the unknown in ourselves, abuse of power.

VIII

STRENGTH.

KEY 9
THE HERMIT

The Hermit stands isolated on a snowy mountain peak, holding up a lantern to guide those below. This is the lighted Lamp of Truth, containing within it the six-pointed star, the Seal of Solomon. The Hermit carries a patriarch's staff to use on the narrow path of initiation. His cloak is the mantle of discretion, and in some decks he partly covers the lantern with it as if to protect Truth from profane eyes.

He is ready to go to the help of every man who cries for Light. He remains on the heights throughout the long nights of spiritual darkness. Only those who dare, do, and keep silent can see the light of the Hermit's lamp. "Be humble, if thou wouldst attain Wisdom; be humbler still when Wisdom thou hast mastered!" (From *The Voice of Silence.*)

The number 9 is the number of pure intellect; also the number of initiation, because it is the trinity of trinities. In it all numbers are gathered up, to emerge once more in a new cycle of ten. The six-pointed star, the Seal of Solomon, is also figured as a 9 by counting the outer and inner points in a special way.

Every Soul is upon some step of the path; we ourselves may have passed them on the way. When we refuse to recognize the Divine Center in others we are bearing false witness, for we are not seeing our fellowmen as they are.

Gautama Buddha has said, "The light of truth's high noon is not for tender leaves," and from the Scriptures come the words of those who have faith, "Thy Word shall be a light unto my path."

Divinatory Meaning: Silent counsel, prudence, discretion. Receiving wisdom from above; instruction from an expert in your field. A meeting with one who will guide the seeker on the path to material or spiritual ends. Attainment of goals. A journey may be necessary in order to gain knowledge.

Reversed: Refusal to listen to wisdom. Immaturity, foolish vices. Rejection of maturity; the tendency to be a perpetual Peter Pan.

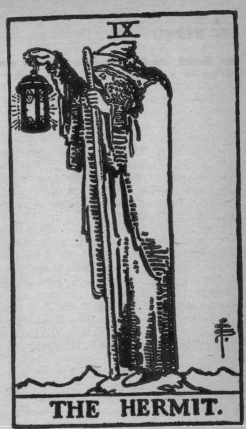

THE HERMIT.

KEY 10
THE WHEEL OF FORTUNE

Here is the ever-turning Wheel of Fortune, which carries men and their destinies up and down. This is the exoteric meaning of the Key, but the many symbols it depicts give it a much more profound and subtle significance.

The Serpent descending the Wheel is Typhon, the Egyptian god of evil, in one of his many forms. Typhon is also used to represent the Life-force on its descent into manifestation. This is the same force that descends at the command of the Magician (Key 1), in the garden. On the right-hand side of the Wheel, the jackal-headed Egyptian god, Hermes-Anubis, is the symbol of intelligence ever aspiring to ascend, while evil is ever descending into darkness and disintegration.

The Wheel has three circles, of which the inner one is the creative force, the middle is the formative power, and the outer is the material world—the same symbolism as in the three tiers of the Hierophant's crown. The eight spokes are like the eight-pointed star in Key 17; they represent universal radiant energy. This design is also repeated ten times on the costume of Key 0, the Fool. The numbers of the four mystical animals in the four corners add up to 26, which is the number of Jehovah, IHVH. These are mentioned in the Bible (Ezekiel 1 : 10; Revelation 4 : 7). There is also a correspondence to the fixed signs of the Zodiac— the bull to Taurus, the lion to Leo, the eagle to Scorpio, the man or angel to Aquarius.

The Sphinx at rest at the top of the Wheel is Wisdom and the principle of equilibration—stability amidst movement, suggesting that we are not always governed by chance and fatality but that we have the power to change our lives.

This Key stands for the perpetual motion of a fluid universe and for the flux of human life within it.

Divinatory Meaning: Success, unexpected turn of luck, change of fortune for the better, new conditions. Creative evolution within the laws of chance.

Reversed: Failure of an enterprise, setbacks. New conditions require courage. You will reap as you have sown.

WHEEL of FORTUNE.

KEY 11
JUSTICE

Justice is seated between the positive and negative forces, indicated by the pillars first seen in the High Priestess and again in the Hierophant. Her sword is lifted in defense of justice, and none can escape it; it points upward, indicating victory, and is two-edged to convey that action destroys as well as builds, that the false must be cut away from the true. The three turrets of her crown and the four sides of the jewel in the center add up to the number 7 (Venus). In her left hand are the scales of gold, always related to balanced judgment. Balance is indicated here, as it is in Key 8, Strength. Keys 8 and 11 represent two aspects of the operation of a single power, creative imagination. All imagination is based on memory.

This key is that of the Great Mother through whose love, care, and perfect justice the children of men may achieve equilibrium.

With this Key, the Fool embarks on a higher cycle of manifestation but with all the experience gained during the previous sequence of ten keys. The purified, disciplined personality now recognizes the One Life and feels it standing beside him, as the sword of power endows him with the ability to divine right from wrong.

Divinatory Meaning: Justice will be done. Balance is required. Lawsuits will be won. The balanced personality demands elimination of excess baggage, wrong ideas, useless forms of education. A mixture of the right ingredients is welcomed—as in science, chemistry, and cooking. May betoken the desire for education, with a well-balanced mind as its objective.

Reversed: Injustice, inequality, legal complications. Advice to use mercy and understanding when judging others, and to avoid excessive tendency to severity.

JUSTICE .

KEY 12
THE HANGED MAN

A youth is suspended by one foot from a T-cross of living wood. His arms, folded behind his back, together with his head, form a triangle with the point downward; his legs form a cross. To an extent, the Hanged Man is still earth-bound, for his foot is attached to the T-cross. He has attained at least a measure of perfection but not yet the complete freedom symbolized in Key 21, the World.

The initiated man now stands as a responsible co-worker with the Divine. It is as though during the cycle from 1 to 10 God had held the hand of His child and guided him in carving the model of the man to be. Now the chisel is left in the hands of the matured youth, and he must create from the materials given him. He must, like the Hermit, take his part in the world's redemption.

The sign ☿ is the sign of the accomplishment of the Great Work—the overcoming of personality and the trans-mutation of the lower passions into pure gold. At the twelfth step we still find the initiate reversed, although ulti-mately he must stand on his own feet and surmount the cross thus: ♃

We see in the Hanged Man the idea of the utter depen-dency of the human personality on the tree of Cosmic Life. Here we also have associations with Hercules as a symbol of the sun in its passage through the 12 signs of the Zodiac or the 12 labors of Hercules. He is a compound of god and hero; he represents the 12 steps of initiation through which every man must pass. Then the lower forces of the signs of the Zodiac will have been transmuted into the higher, up-lifting powers of each sign.

This card has profound significance, even though much of it is veiled. Man must now accomplish his regeneration for himself consciously and voluntarily.

Divinatory Meaning: In spiritual matters, wisdom, pro-phetic power. A pause in one's life, suspended decisions. Self-surrender leads to the transformation of the personality. Material temptation is conquered.

XII

THE HANGED MAN.

Reversed: Arrogance, preoccupation with the ego, resistance to spiritual influences. Absorption in physical matters. Wasted effort. False prophecy.

KEY 13
DEATH

A skeleton in armor rides a white horse that tramples over a fallen king and draws near to a child and a woman, who turn from him in dread. The standing figure is a bishop in a miter shaped like a fish—denoting the Piscean Age (which is about to end). Death carries a banner on which there is a five-petaled rose, symbol of Mars and the Life-force. The river in the background indicates the constant circulation of the Life-force into materialization and out again. The water, as it flows to the sea, is sucked up by the sun to form clouds, from which rain falls into the streams and then to the river again. The sun on the eastern horizon indicates immortality—once the two towers (which we meet again in Key 18) have been passed.

The fundamental meaning of Death in Key 13 is that of the Manifestor of the Universe. The sun is the center and the 12 signs of the Zodiac surround it, making 13 signs in all. The king has fallen, reminding us that kings must inevitably fall. There is perpetual transformation, one aspect of which is death-birth. Death is a protest against stagnation—it is by death that social changes for the better come to pass and old ideas give way. With the new generation, new ideas gain currency as youth moves into maturity.

This card is a suggestion to change old concepts for new, to change rigid intellectual patterns. Petty prejudices, ambitions, and opinions gradually die. The change from the personal to the universal view is so radical that mystics often compare it to death. But Death is the twin brother of Life. Creation necessitates its opposite—destruction. As Spirit descends into matter, so it must return to its source. Death is half of the Universal Transforming Principle. But Spirit is immortal; thus humanity can never die, for the Destroyer has become the Creator.

Divinatory Meaning: Transformation, change, destruction followed by renewal. The change may be in consciousness. Birth of new ideas, new opportunities.

Reversed: Disaster, political upheaval, revolution, anarchy. Death of a political figure. Temporary stagnation. Tendency to inertia.

DEATH.

KEY 14
TEMPERANCE

This Key represents the archangel Michael, who is related
to fire and the sun. He pours the essence of life from the
silver cup of the subconscious into the golden cup of the
conscious, from the unseen into the seen and then back
again. This depicts the entry of Spirit into matter and the
influence of matter upon Spirit, as well as the flowing of
the past through the present and into the future.

The square on the breast of the angel indicates the four-
square reality of physical manifestation, and within it the
triangle of Spirit points upward. (This symbol is also the
sign of the sacred book of the Tarot.) Four plus 3 equals 7,
indicating the aspects of Divine Life and the seven chakras
or centers of the body used in yoga meditation. Note that
one foot rests on earth and the other in the water, to symbolize that the archangel is equally at home in the conscious or the subconscious. The water in the pool indicates
the subconscious mind of man and the universe. On the
bank of the pool are irises, a reminder that Iris was the
Greek goddess of the rainbow. At the end of the path there
is the crown of mastery and attainment.

This is the card of vibration, or radiant energy, of the
tempering and modification of experience. Just as Key 4,
the Emperor, is the foundation of the physical, so Key 14
is the foundation of the mind—adding to 4 the power of 10.
Here Man has, in large measure, mastered his own thoughts
and achieved mental balance. There is nothing in the cosmos
but vibration, and all forms of vibration can be modified
and managed by the adept. But we do nothing of ourselves
alone. Our guardian angel makes the tests and trials that
lead us along the path of attainment.

As we learn to transfer the Life-force from the imagination (moon) into the activity of the conscious (sun), the
will is developed and the imagination purified so that in
pouring from the silver cup to the golden one we lose nothing. This is another of the stages of occult progress that
the Fool must take on the path to mastery.

Divinatory Meaning: Adaptation, tempering, coordination,
self-control, modification. Working in harmony with others,

good management. What we have imagined will come to pass. Successful combinations will be achieved.

Reversed: Competing interests, unfortunate combinations. Quarreling, corruption, separation. Possibility of shipwreck or some other disaster.

KEY 15
THE DEVIL

The Devil is the polar opposite of the Archangel in Key 14. His horns are those of a goat, and his face is a goat's face; he has bat wings and donkey ears that suggest the obstinacy and stubbornness of materialism.

He sits on a half-cube, which signifies the half-knowledge of what is only the visible, sensory side of reality. His right hand is upraised, giving the sign of black magic, as opposed to the Hierophant's, which is raised in blessing. On the palm is the symbol of Saturn, the planet of limitation and inertia.

In his left hand he holds the smoldering torch of destruction; the inverted pentagram, denoting evil intent, is inscribed above his forehead. Chained to the half-cube are two nude figures similar to those in Key 6. The tail of the man represents the wrong use of the signs of the Zodiac; the woman's tail resembles a bunch of grapes, suggesting the wrong use of the wine of life.

There is no Devil except of man's own creation, and here it is evident that men are chained by their own wrong choices. However, the chains about their necks are loose and can be removed at will.

Divinatory Meaning: Black magic, discontent, depression. Illness. Wrong use of force. Bondage to the material; sensation divorced from understanding.

Reversed: The beginning of spiritual understanding. Removing the chains of bondage to the material. Timidity, failure to make decisions. The overcoming of pride and self-interest.

XV

THE DEVIL .

KEY 16
THE TOWER

This is the Tower of ambition built on false premises. It is made of the bricks of traditional race-thought and the wrong use of personal will. Streaks of lightning issue from the Sun; the crown of materialistic thought falls from the Tower. The lightning is also the Divine fire that destroys only what is evil and purifies and refines what is good. The falling drops of light or dew, seen here as well as in Key 18 and in the Aces of three suits of the Minor Arcana, are Hebrew *Yods*. They signify the descent of the Life-force from above into the conditions of material existence. The man and woman are falling from their tower of material security, after a brilliant glimpse of Truth.

We see here the Cosmic Consciousness struggling to break through man's thoughts of material ambition and bring them to naught in order that he may build again. When man sells his soul to the devil and uses his occult knowledge for evil ends, then destruction descends upon him from above.

Key 16 has been associated with the fall of Satan's kingdom. This tower is built upon a foundation of mis-apprehension. "Except the Lord build the house, they labor in vain that build it."

Divinatory Meaning: Change, conflict, catastrophe. Overthrow of existing ways of life, old notions upset. Disruption will bring enlightenment in its wake. Selfish ambition is about to come to naught. Bankruptcy.

Reversed: The gain of freedom of body or mind at great cost. False accusations, false imprisonment, oppression.

THE TOWER.

KEY 17
THE STAR

A beautiful maiden kneels with one knee on the land and one foot in the water. The earth supports her weight, but she balances herself on the water of the subconscious. She is the Empress and Mother Nature pouring the waters of life onto the material earth. The five rivulets represent the five senses before they run into the pool of the Universal Consciousness. From the other pitcher she pours directly into the pool, which is stirred into vibration by meditation.

Behind the maiden the sacred ibis of thought rests on a tree (mind). In the sky are seven small eight-pointed stars and a large one, all representing radiant cosmic energy. The seven smaller stars correspond to the seven chakras of the body.

This is the key of meditation, showing us that meditation modifies and transmutes the personal expressions of cosmic energy that pour down upon the maiden. If we will but listen, the Truth will unveil itself to us in the silence. From the record of nature's memory, symbolized by the scroll of the High Priestess, we gain wisdom, out of which meditation develops specific powers by controlling the animal forces in human personality—as pictured in Key 8.

Divinatory Meaning: Insight, inspiration, hope. Unselfish aid. Good health. The gifts of the Spirit. Great love will be given and received.

Reversed: Pessimism, doubt, stubbornness, lack of perception. Chance of physical or mental illness.

KEY 18
THE MOON

The Moon in three phases watches over the landscape. From the pool of Cosmic Mind stuff in the foreground, a crayfish appears, symbolizing the early stages of conscious unfoldment. The wolf is nature's untamed creation; the dog is the result of adaptation to life with man. In the background, halfway up the path, are the twin towers Man has erected to protect himself from his hostile environment. The Moon will lead him along the rugged path, past the towers, to the final heights of attainment, if he will be guided by her reflected light and listen to the voice of his subconscious. Once again, the falling drops are *Yods*, representing the descent of the Life-force from above into material existence.

This is the key of sleep and dreams. The Moon's three phases of intuition concern body, mind, and spirit. The Moon Mother watches over the birth of Spirit into material manifestation. The number 18 consists of the digits 1 and 8, which add up to 9, thus becoming the second 9 and indicating the second initiation. The Hermit was the first 9 on the path.

The Fool is still on his journey—learning, falling back, and then again advancing.

Divinatory Meaning: Intuition, imagination, deception. Unfoldment of latent psychic powers. Unforeseen perils, secret foes. Bad luck for one you love.

Reversed: Imagination will be harnessed by practical considerations. Storms will be weathered, peace gained at a cost. No risk should be taken.

KEY 19
THE SUN

A naked child rides a white horse and holds a red banner aloft. The horse is solar energy, which he now controls without saddle or bridle. He represents perfect control between the conscious and the unconscious. His red banner signifies action and vibration, as do the rays of the Sun—so different from the quiet, reflected light of the Moon. He carries the banner in his left hand to indicate that control has now passed from the conscious (right hand) into the subconscious (left hand)—just as, while we are learning to play the piano or ride a bicycle, we use the conscious part of our minds, but when we have learned, we pass control over to the subconscious. The expert pianist can carry on a conversation while playing an intricate piece, and the youthful bicyclist shouts, "Look, Ma, no hands."

The walled garden behind the child is the cultivated garden of Man, which he has left behind him. There are four sunflowers looking toward him for their full development, instead of toward the sun. They represent the four elements—Air, Earth, Fire, and Water.

The child is fair, like the Fool, and, like the Fool, he wears a wreath and a red feather. His nakedness indicates that he no longer has anything to hide. Here the Fool has gained spiritual victory over the lower aspects of his nature—a very different triumph from that which he was demonstrating as the Charioteer in Key 7, when his conquest was only over his own will.

The number 19 is associated in mythology and legends as the number of the Sun. One who has attained to 19 becomes a Sun initiate, ready to accomplish for humanity on the inner planes what the Sun accomplishes in giving light and warmth to the earth.

Divinatory Meaning: Material happiness, success, attainment. A good marriage. Happy reunions. Achievements in the arts, science, and agriculture. Studies completed; liberation. Pleasure in the simple life.

Reversed: Future plans clouded, trouble in marriage, a broken engagement, possible loss of a job or home.

THE SUN .

KEY 20
JUDGMENT

The angel Gabriel emerges from the heavens blowing on his bannered trumpet, its seven basic tones indicated by the seven lines radiating from it. This imperious blast is the creative Word that liberates Man from his terrestrial limitations. The cross on the banner is the solar symbol of the balance of forces. The coffins float on the sea of Cosmic Mind stuff, which is the ultimate goal of those streams and pools that began in the High Priestess and passed through many forms. Snowy mountains beyond the sea are the heights of abstract thought.

"The hour cometh and now is in which all they which are in the tombs [of human belief] shall hear his voice and shall arise."

This is the reawakening of Nature under the influence of Spirit, the mystery of birth in death. The man arising from the tomb of world belief is again the conscious, the woman the subconscious, the child the regenerated personality. Spirit has now fully clothed itself in Man, the Word has been made flesh and dwells amongst us. The one who has passed the tests (including the crucial last test) is always called the "twice-born."

Key 20 is composed of two complete cycles of 10, each containing the experience of the 9 digits. But unlike the first 10, in which 1 stands before the 0 of unmanifest forces, here we find 2, signifying that the Life-force entered into matter and was multiplied.

"The Power belongs to him who knows," and he who knows is then responsible. Therefore the Fool is the one who by effort and suffering has found the secrets of life.

Divinatory Meaning: A life well lived, a work well done. Awakening, renewal. Legal judgments in one's favor. A change of personal consciousness, which is now on the verge of blending with the universal.

Reversed: Weakness, disillusion. Fear of death; failure to find happiness. Separation, divorce. Possible loss of worldly goods.

JUDGEMENT.

KEY 21
THE WORLD

Here we see a dancer clad only in a scarf. An oval wreath frames her figure, symbolizing the mystery of creation. The ribbons twined around the wreath again suggest the cosmic lemniscate. The four beasts at the four corners of the key, a slightly different version of those in Key 10, represent the four elements of Air, Fire, Water, and Earth, which have here been balanced and become the cornerstones of life.

The legs of the dancer form a cross, as do those of the Hanged Man, but the triangle he represented was under the cross, signifying that he was still bound by earthly things. Here, a triangle is formed pointing upward from the dancer's hands to the top of her head. Thus the triangle of Spirit now surmounts the cross of the material $\triangle\!\!\!+$. The dancer's two wands represent the powers of involution and evolution, which she now possesses.

Though the dancer seems a female, some writers claim that a hermaphrodite is depicted in this Key, with the veil hiding the truth. This is thought by some to be the ideal state from which humanity came and to which it returns. This attainment is the merging of the self-conscious with the subconscious, and the blending of these two with the superconscious—the final state of Cosmic Consciousness, the supreme goal to which all the other keys have led.

Divinatory Meaning: Completion, reward, success, triumph in all undertakings. Travel, change of residence, arrival at a state of Cosmic Consciousness. The path of liberation.

Reversed: Success yet to be won; fear of change or travel, too great an attachment to one's place of residence or job. Lack of vision.

THE WORLD.

THE MINOR ARCANA

The Minor Arcana are believed by some to be of even more ancient origin than the Major Arcana. Since both had already been combined into one pack at the time when Court de Gébelin brought them to public attention, there is no way of confirming or disproving this supposition. Indeed, there are some writers on the subject who disregard the Minor Arcana, concentrating entirely on the Major Arcana—especially as they relate to the Tree of Life of the Kabalah. Continued research, however, reveals that the meanings of the Minor Arcana show an unmistakable correspondence to those of the ten Sephiroth of the Tree of Life. (This relationship will be discussed in the section on the Tarot and the Kabalah.)

A. E. Waite's Rider Pack was chosen for this book because it was the only pack we could find that had an illustration for each of the 56 cards of the Minor Arcana. The mind more easily retains the memory of the meaning of a card after one has looked at a graphic representation rather than at merely the number of symbols in a design—say, three Pentacles, nine Swords, or six Cups.

The universe, it has been said, was created from four basic elements: Fire, Water, Air, and Earth, corresponding to the four Hebrew letters IHVH (Jehovah). In ancient Hebrew there were no written vowels, and these letters represented forms of the verb "to be," used with *that,* not *he,* for the letters IHVH are a symbol for the Conscious Energy that brings all things and all creatures into existence. "I" stands for the element Fire, "H" for Water, "V" for Air, the life breath, and the final "H" for the solidity of the element Earth.

The four suits of the Minor Arcana—Wands, Cups, Swords, and Pentacles—also correspond with IHVH and the four elements, so we have:

I	Fire	Wands
H	Water	Cups
V	Air	Swords
H	Earth	Pentacles

Each suit is made up of cards numbered from ace to ten, plus four Court cards: King, Queen, Knight, and Page. The Tarot, as has been mentioned, was the forerunner of the modern deck. If the Knights were left out and the suit names changed (Wands to clubs, Cups to hearts, Swords to spades, and Pentacles to diamonds), what remained would be virtually identical with our modern playing cards. Another similarity has already been noted: the complete deck of 78 cards contains an unnumbered card called the Fool, from which has evolved today's Joker, also unnumbered. The four suits of the Minor Arcana are represented by the four animals of the Apocalypse (see description in Keys 10 and 21 of the Major Arcana).

Wands

This suit indicates animation and enterprise, energy and growth. The wands depicted in the cards are always in leaf, suggesting the constant renewal of life and growth. The associations are with the world of ideas, also with creation in all its forms, including agriculture. The salamander is the animal associated with Wands. In the theory of Paracelsus (1493–1541), the salamander was a being who inhabited the element fire. Among the animals of the Apocalypse, Wands are synonymous with lions. The direction assigned to Wands is south; the temperament of Wand people is sanguine. This is the suit of the laborer.

Cups

This suit generally betokens love and happiness. The cups

in the cards refer to water, a symbol of the subconscious mind, the instincts, and the emotions of love and pleasure, the good life, fertility, and beauty. The animal—or rather, creature—for Cups is the undine, a female water spirit. The direction is west; the temperament is phlegmatic. The Apocalypse figure is the Water Carrier, Aquarius. This is the suit of the priest.

Swords

The swords generally express aggression, strife, boldness, and courage. But sometimes they can mean hatred, battle, and enemies. This is the suit of misfortune and disaster. Its direction is north; its creature is the sylph, an elemental being of the air. The Sword temperament is said to be melancholy, and the Apocalypse figure is the eagle. This is the suit of the warriors.

Pentacles

The symbols on the cards are called pentacles, which in ancient times were metal disks inscribed with magic formulas. In this suit the pentacles are inscribed with the five-pointed star called the pentagram—a symbol of the magic arts and the five senses of man, the five elements of Nature, and the five extremities of the human body. Here, they represent money, acquisition of fortune, trade. The direction is east, the temperament bilious. The creature here is the gnome, a being of the earth. The Apocalypse figure is the bull. This is the suit of the merchants.

The Wands

ACE of WANDS.

*ACE
OF
WANDS*

A hand comes out of a cloud, offering a flowering wand; eight detached leaves float in the air, suggesting Hebrew *Yods* or the descent of spirit into matter. Aces signify beginnings; Wands, animation and enterprise. Therefore, something of a creative nature is being offered to the Querent.

Divinatory Meaning: Beginning of an enterprise, invention, or the beginning of a family. Perhaps the beginning of a journey, an adventure, an escapade.

Reversed: Canceling of new enterprise, journey deferred, clouded joy, false starts.

TWO
OF
WANDS

The Lord of Dominion looks from his battlements out over the sea. He holds a globe in his right hand and a staff in his left; another staff is held by a iron ring. Roses, signifying desire, are mixed with the lilies of pure thought, forming a cross with equal arms. This suggests that there is a balance here between thought and desire.

Divinatory Meaning: Boldness, courage in embarking on an enterprise. The employment of scientific methods. Influence over another. Kindness and generosity—yet a proud and unforgiving nature.

Reversed: Restlessness, obstinacy, fear, physical suffering. The good beginning has turned against the Querent.

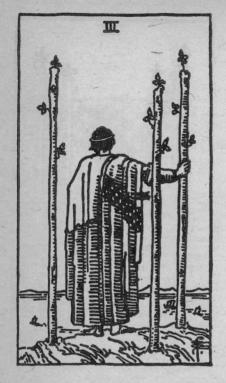

**THREE
OF
WANDS**

Here is the established merchant looking out to sea, as his ships come into port. He has accomplished what the man in the Two of Wands was just beginning.

Divinatory Meaning: Realization of hope, established strength, nobility, wealth, power. Caution against pride and arrogance. Partnership. Help will be offered by a successful merchant.

Reversed: Beware of help offered. Wealth may slip away. There may be treachery and disappointment.

**FOUR
OF
WANDS**

Bouquets of flowers are held high by two rejoicing maidens. A garland of celebration swings from the tops of four flowering wands. In the background is a castle with moat.

Divinatory Meaning: Perfected work; rest after labor. Peace, prosperity, harmony. Romance, a coming marriage.

Reversed: Though the meaning remains the same, there will not be quite the same fullness of peace, prosperity, and success.

FIVE
OF
WANDS

Five youths are fighting with huge wands. Are they in earnest? Since the fives in each of the four suits are negative, we can assume this is a serious quarrel. Remember, Wands mean enterprise, energy, but the five signifies that this energy is used negatively.

Divinatory Meaning: Violent strife, rashness, competition. In the battle of life, boldness changes things for the better. Obstacles. Lawsuit.

Reversed: Generosity. New business opportunities. Victory after surmounting obstacles.

SIX
OF
WANDS

This is the Lord of Victory, who comes riding by, carrying a laurel crown on his stave. His men are marching beside him.

Divinatory Meaning: Good news. Victory after strife. Pleasure gained through labor. Success through industry. Advancement in the arts and sciences. Friends are helpful.

Reversed: Rewards are delayed. Insolence of the victorious. Watch for successful enemy.

**SEVEN
OF
WANDS**

The youth's stance is that of a yeoman fighting for his
land. Six enemies are attacking from below.

Divinatory Meaning: Victory through courage. Success
against opposition. The Querent has the position of advantage. Competition in business or trade. Certain success.

Reversed: Ignorance, pretense. The Querent is threatened.
Caution against indecision.

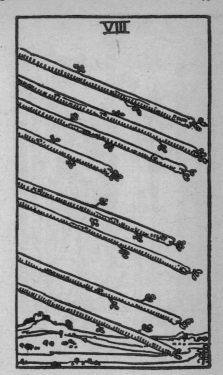

EIGHT
OF
WANDS

Having sped through open country, these eight wands are about to come to rest, their energy spent.

Divinatory Meaning: Great haste, great hope, too rapid advancement. That which is on the move. Hasty communication. Messages, letters of love. Approach to a goal. Journey by air.

Reversed: Delay, stagnation in business or affairs of the heart. Arrows of jealousy.

**NINE
OF
WANDS**

His bandaged head indicates the man has already fought and is prepared to fight again. The staves behind him suggest the boundary of that which he protects.

Divinatory Meaning: The pause in a struggle. Preparedness, strength in reserve. Eventual victory but steady force must be applied. Obstinacy, strength, power, health.

Reversed: Weakness, ill health, adversity, displeasure, obstacles to be overcome.

*TEN
OF
WANDS*

Here the young man is carrying ten staves, and the burden seems almost more than he can manage, yet he staggers on toward the city.

Divinatory Meaning: Force and energy applied to selfish ends. Power unwisely used. Carrying a burden of ill-regulated power. Here is also a refining test by fire, the heart tried by pain. Problem soon to be solved.

Reversed: Intrigues, separation, emigration. If a lawsuit is pending, there will be some loss.

PAGE
OF WANDS

Some call the Pages princesses, and certainly from the picture this could be either a youth or a maiden who stands there boldly upholding a wand as if about to deliver a message. Three pyramids in the background are symbolic of the earth in its maternal aspect, and are also related to fire (as is the entire suit of Wands).

This card should be chosen to represent a boy or girl of fair complexion, since Wands always indicate blonds with blue or hazel eyes.

Divinatory Meaning: Courage, beauty. A nature sudden in love or anger. Desire for power; enthusiasm. A messenger or postman. A bearer of tidings. If this card appears in a spread next to one representing a man, there will be favorable testimony concerning him.

Reversed: Cruel, unstable, domineering. If you are a woman, he may break your heart. Announcing bad news.

PAGE of WANDS.

KNIGHT
OF WANDS

A handsome young knight in armor gallops across the plains. There are three pyramids in the distance. His mantle is decorated with salamanders biting their tails. Salamanders supposedly can go through fire without being burned, and wands symbolize fire.

This card is to be chosen to represent a Querent in early manhood, with blond hair and blue or hazel eyes.

Divinatory Meaning: A young man, possibly a warrior, filled with energy. He can be a generous friend or lover, but is also likely to be cruel and brutal. He is hasty in all he does.

May also mean change of residence, emigration, quick departure. Knights in a spread may also mean the coming or going of a matter.

Reversed: The would-be lover turns jealous, creates conflict. Discord, frustration, lack of energy. Work interfered with.

KNIGHT of WANDS.

QUEEN
OF WANDS

A crowned queen sits on her throne, holding a staff in her right hand. In her left there is a sunflower, signifying nature and her control over it. The arms of her throne are lions' heads, to indicate she also controls the lower forces of animal nature. In the foreground there is a black cat, the sinister aspect of Venus. A tapestry hangs behind the Queen, repeating the theme of lions and sunflowers; the three pyramids are seen again.

Choose this card for a blonde, with blue or hazel eyes.

Divinatory Meaning: She has great power to attract that which she wants, and is fruitful in mind and body. Loving nature and her home, she is practical with money and sound in her business judgments.

If she does not represent a woman, then she represents these qualities: success in undertakings; love of home and growing things; kindness and generosity.

Reversed: Domineering, obstinate, revengeful; likely to turn suddenly against another without cause. If married, she could be unfaithful.

QUEEN of WANDS.

KING
OF WANDS

He sits in royal robes, a crown upon his head. Lions and salamanders adorn the pillar behind him, and the design of his mantle is made up of salamanders. There is a little salamander seated beside him. All these signify fire. Wands also represent the scepter of the king and the magician's rod of power that can conjure the elementals and utilize their forces for either spiritual or material gain.

This is the card to represent a blond man with blue or hazel eyes—a mature man of enterprise.

Divinatory Meaning: Handsome and passionate, he is agile in mind and body. A country gentleman, generally married. Loyal and noble, he comes of good family. Sometimes he is too hasty.

If no man seems to be involved in the spread of cards, you will find these traits: honesty, friendliness, passion. The card may mean unexpected heritage; a good marriage.

Reversed: Intolerant, prejudiced, ill-natured. High-principled to a fault. Severe and ruthless.

KING of WANDS

The Cups

ACE
OF
CUPS

ACE ♣ CUPS.

Again a hand comes forth from a cloud, offering a cup
from which five streams of living water fall into the lake
below—a symbol of the subconscious mind. A dove of peace
holds a wafer marked with a cross, and the dew of Spirit
descends from the cup onto the water lilies, symbols (like
the lotus) signifying eternal life.

Divinatory Meaning: The beginning of great love. Joy,
contentment. Productiveness, fertility. Beauty and pleasure.
A reminder that when the mind is filled with Spirit, the
Spirit will fill the material cup to overflowing.

Reversed: False love. Clouded joy. Instability. Hesitancy
to nurture love.

TWO
OF
CUPS

A young man and maiden make their vows of affection, each holding a cup filled with the good things of life. Two serpents entwine a staff, the phallic emblem of life's creative fire. The serpents represent a balance between good and evil; above them the lion of carnal desires has taken wing.

Divinatory Meaning: Harmony of the masculine and the feminine. Reciprocity, the beginning of a friendship or love affair. Balance of ideas and plans with a kindred soul.

Reversed: False love, dissipation, folly, violent passion, disunity, misunderstanding.

THREE
OF
CUPS

Maidens in a fertile garden raise their cups high in congratulation on the conclusion of a matter in prosperity.

Divinatory Meaning: Success, abundance. Good luck, fortune, victory. Happy issue of an undertaking. Hospitality. Pleasure.

Reversed: Too much sensuality, overindulgence in food and drink. Pleasure turns to pain, success to ashes.

**FOUR
OF
CUPS**

A young man sits in contemplation under a tree, oblivious of the three filled cups before him. From above he is offered another cup, which he also disdains.

Divinatory Meaning: A stationary period in one's life; weariness, surfeit. Dissatisfaction with material success. Re-evaluation of one's earthly pleasures. Kindness from others.

Reversed: Waking from a period of contentment or contemplation. New relationships now possible. New goals, new ambition.

**FIVE
OF
CUPS**

Wrapped in the black cloak of despair, the figure contemplates the three spilled cups as the wine of pleasure sinks into the ground. Two more cups behind him remain to be taken, but he ignores them. In the distance a bridge leads to a small castle. The river is the stream of the subconscious.

Divinatory Meaning: Disappointment. Sorrow in those things from which pleasure was expected. Disillusionments in love. Marriage broken up. Loss of friendship. Vain regret; loss, but with something left over.

Reversed: Return of enjoyment. New alliances formed. Return of an old friend or loved one. Hopeful expectations.

*SIX
OF
CUPS*

In a village green, a little boy offers a girl a cup filled with flowers. The cottage in the background conveys thoughts of home and happy childhood memories. Five more flower-filled cups are arranged nearby.

Divinatory Meaning: Happiness, enjoyment, but coming from the past. Meeting with a childhood acquaintance. Pleasant memories. Or this card may mean new friendships. A gift from an admirer. New knowledge and new opportunities.

Reversed: Living too much in the past. Clinging to outworn morals and manners. Worthless associates. Possibility of an inheritance or gift from the past.

SEVEN
OF
CUPS

A man in black stands amazed at the fantastic visions that rise out of the seven cups in the clouds before him—a castle, jewels, the wreath of victory with a skull below it, the red dragon of temptation, the head of a fair woman, the serpent of jealousy, and the covered figure of the man's own angel, shimmering with divine light.

Divinatory Meaning: Dreams, castles in the air, an imagination that has been working overtime. The seeker's forces have been too scattered. Illusionary success. Selfish dissipation; deception.

Reversed: Good resolutions. Slight success must be followed up. New will and determination. Intelligent selection.

**EIGHT
OF
CUPS**

A man with a pilgrim's staff is abandoning his success, as exemplified by the eight neatly stacked cups. A barren scene lies before him, and there is a moon, both full and in its declining aspect, looking on.

Divinatory Meaning: Things thrown aside as soon as gained. Journeying from place to place. Misery and repining without cause. Disappointment in love. The seeker may desire to leave material success for something higher. Success abandoned.

Reversed: Interest in success. Joy, feasting, a new love. The spiritual abandoned for the material.

**NINE
OF
CUPS**

This is the wish card. If the Nine of Cups comes up in a Querent's spread, he will get his wish. The picture here is of a well-fed, well-satisfied man who has neatly arranged all nine of the cups of plenty in a row behind him.

Divinatory Meaning: Material success, satisfaction. All the good things of life are available. The Querent will get his wish. Physical well-being.

Reversed: Misplaced reliance; false freedom. There may be some deprivation or illness, or overindulgence in food and drink. The Querent's wish will not be fulfilled.

TEN
OF
CUPS

A young couple and their dancing children, with their
home in the background, hold up their arms in joy over
the rainbow's promise.

Divinatory Meaning: Contentment. Lasting happiness because it is inspired from above rather than being the sensual
satisfaction indicated in the Nine of Cups. Perfection of
human love. Great friendship. Lasting success. Peacemaking.

Reversed: Loss of friendship. Betrayal. Wantonness, waste.
Criminal satisfactions.

PAGE
OF CUPS

A well-dressed youth or maiden stands contemplating a cup from which a fish emerges—a symbol of the appearance of an idea in the imagination. In the background is the sea. In the Cups, the suit of the subconscious, water in some form is found in many of the cards.

This is the card to choose if you are reading for a youth or a girl under eighteen or a young person still unmarried—with light-brown hair and hazel eyes.

Divinatory Meaning: A melancholy and passionate youth, studious but given to flights of imagination. Willing to render service to the Querent.

If this card does not signify a youth, it will mean the Querent is drawn to the arts, is given to meditation. News, a message, perhaps the birth of a child. New business methods proposed.

Reversed: Little desire to create. Dilettantism. Good taste. Seduction. A deception may soon be uncovered. Obstacles. Unpleasant news.

PAGE of CUPS.

KNIGHT
OF CUPS

A stately Knight in armor, but not warlike. He wears a winged helmet, sign of the imagination and of the dual-sexed nature of Hermes. He carries his cup firmly as he approaches a stream.

This is a card to choose for a young man with light-brown hair and hazel eyes.

Divinatory Meaning: A young man who is graceful, poetic, but indolent. He is a dreamer of sensual delights. Can mean the bringer of a message, a proposition, an invitation.

Reversed: Sensual, idle, untruthful. Swindling, trickery, fraud. Propositions should be carefully looked into.

KNIGHT of CUPS.

QUEEN
OF CUPS

A queen sits on a throne decorated with undines (water nymphs), and surrounded by water. Beautiful, fair, and dreamy, she contemplates a cup shaped like a eucharistic emblem, after the manner of a ciborium. The cup is closed, signifying that what it contains is not to be seen by all.

Choose this card for a woman with light-brown hair and hazel eyes.

Divinatory Meaning: A woman who is able to put into practice what her visions decree. She is the good wife and mother—honest, devoted, and loyal.

If the Querent does not recognize such a woman in his or her life, then someone with vision should be considered, or someone who is kind though not willing to take too much trouble for another. Success, happiness, pleasure are indicated.

Reversed: A perverse character. Intelligent but not to be relied on. Dishonesty. Immorality.

QUEEN of CUPS.

KING
OF CUPS

A king sits on his throne surrounded by a rather turbulent sea. A fish leaps out of the water, and there is a ship in the distance. The king holds his scepter in one hand, a large cup in the other. A golden fish is suspended from a chain around his neck. He represents balance and peace, arts and science.

This card should be chosen for a man with light-brown hair and hazel eyes.

Divinatory Meaning: This man is skilled in both law and trade. He may be connected with either a church or a worldly institution. He is kind and considerate and willing to take responsibility.

If such a man is not indicated, then look for traits of liberality, generosity, consideration, creative intelligence, and interest in arts and religion.

Reversed: A powerful man, but likely to be crafty and violent. A fierce nature under a calm exterior. Double dealing. Beware of being robbed of either virtue or money.

KING of CUPS.

The Swords

ACE of SWORDS.

*ACE
OF
SWORDS*

A two-edged sword is held by a hand that emerges from the clouds. Its point is encircled by a crown of victory. An olive branch (mercy) and a palm branch (severity) hang from it. Around the sword are six Hebrew *Yods*, recalling the six days of the Mosaic creation. The card symbolizes Justice, which maintains the world order, the equilibrium of mercy and severity.

Divinatory Meaning: Conquest, triumph of power, great activity. The power to love strongly or to hate. Possible birth of a child who will be of heroic temperament. Championship.

Reversed: Conquest, but the results are disastrous. Obstacles, great loss, infertility.

TWO
OF
SWORDS

A seated woman balances two swords on her shoulders. The old cartomancers described her as "hoodwinked"—we would say "blindfolded." Perhaps she is blind to her situation. Behind her the sea contains rocks to trap the unwary. A new moon shines down upon her.

Divinatory Meaning: Tension in relationships. Indecision. Balanced forces. Military friendships. A well-developed sense of balance and rhythm but needing direction. Stalemate.

Reversed: Release, movement of affairs, sometimes in the wrong direction. Avoid impostors. Sympathy for those in trouble. Disloyalty.

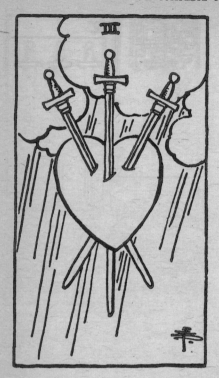

**THREE
OF
SWORDS**

A heart pierced by three swords is seen against a stormy sky.

Divinatory Meaning: Stormy weather for the affections. Tears, separation, quarreling. A general upheaval of the environment. Possibility of civil war. Political strife.

Reversed: There is still confusion, loss, sorrow, upheaval, but in lesser degree.

**FOUR
OF
SWORDS**

In a church with a stained-glass window, the effigy of a knight lies full length upon his tomb. His hands are clasped together in prayer.

Divinatory Meaning: Hermit's repose. Rest after war. Banishment. Relaxation of anxiety, release from suffering. There will soon be a change for the better. Not a card of death.

Reversed: Renewed activity; qualified success. Movement in one's affairs; social unrest. A caution to be wise, circumspect, and economical.

**FIVE
OF
SWORDS**

A knave has captured the swords of his adversaries, who depart in dejection. Storm clouds fill the sky. The Querent may be either the conquered or the conqueror, depending on the cards next to this one in the spread.

Divinatory Meaning: Failure, defeat. Degradation. Conquest of others. Unfairness, slander, cruelty, cowardliness.

Reversed: Beware of pride. There is a chance of loss or defeat. Attendance at a funeral. Empty victory. Sorrow. Weakness.

SIX
OF
SWORDS

In a state of dejection, a woman and child are ferried across the water to a calm shore.

Divinatory Meaning: The future will be better. Success after anxieties. Journey to a new home, by water. Sending someone to represent you in an undertaking. Also a journey in consciousness.

Reversed: You will stay where you are. No immediate way out of present difficulties. Unfavorable issue of a law-suit or other undertaking.

**SEVEN
OF
SWORDS**

A man is seen in the act of stealing away, carrying five swords from the military camp in the background. Two swords are still left impaled in the ground.

Divinatory Meaning: A plan that may fail. An unwise attempt to make away with what is not yours. Unstable effort. Arguments over plans. Spying on another. Partial success.

Reversed: Possibility of unexpected good. Sound advice. Instruction. Wishes about to be fulfilled.

**EIGHT
OF
SWORDS**

Again a maiden is "hoodwinked" (blindfolded), and this time she is also bound. She stands in a marshy place surrounded by swords. In the distance there is a castle high on a rocky cliff.

Divinatory Meaning: Narrow or restricted surroundings. Bondage. Imprisonment through indecision. Betrayal. Fear to move out of a situation. Temporary sickness.

Reversed: New beginnings now possible. Impulsive, generous nature. Relaxation from fear. Freedom.

NINE OF SWORDS

Awakening from sleep in the dead of night, a woman sits in despair, her head in her hands. Zodiacal signs decorate her coverlet. Nine swords hang heavy over her head.

Divinatory Meaning: Suffering, loss, misery. Burden, oppression. Doubt and desolation. Illness. May mean death of a loved one.

Reversed: Patience, unselfishness. Time brings healing. Tomorrow is another day.

TEN
OF
SWORDS

The swords in the other cards of this suit merely surrounded the person; here they have actually pierced him. He lies in a desolate waste, a black sky above him.

Divinatory Meaning: Though the Nine of Swords showed despair, the meaning here is even more serious. Ruin of plans and projects. Defeat in war. Disruption of home life. Tears will fall. Trouble will come in spite of riches and high position. Not a card of violent death. A suggestion to give charity freely to those in trouble.

Reversed: Overthrow of evil forces. Some success and profit. Courage to rise again. In spiritual matters, looking to higher powers for help.

PAGE
OF SWORDS

A youth (or maiden) holds a sword with both hands while walking swiftly over rough terrain. The wild clouds and the flight of a flock of birds give the feeling that trouble is brewing. The Swords are the cards of warriors, of strife and misfortune.

Choose this card for an energetic boy or girl with brown hair and brown eyes.

Divinatory Meaning: A young person who might be a page in the diplomatic or government service. He or she already has great understanding and knows how to use diplomacy.

This card can also mean a message and certain types of spying, as well as grace and dexterity.

Reversed: Impostor, likely to be exposed. Frivolity and cunning. Possibility of ill health. Be prepared for the unexpected.

PAGE of SWORDS.

KNIGHT
OF SWORDS

Here a knight dashes across open country, perhaps on a mission of romantic chivalry. Storm clouds are in the sky; cypress trees, sacred to Venus, are blown by the wind. Swords are the suit of air—thus we see birds, one on the knight's arm, another on his mantle at the knee, and more of them on the horse's harness. They are companioned by butterflies, symbols of the soul. Note that the swords in this suit point either upward to the highest ideals of life or downward to the depths of despair and death.

Choose this card for a dark-haired, brown-eyed young man.

Divinatory Meaning: A dashing, brave young man. Though he may be domineering, he has a clean heart and is full of courage. The card may also mean the coming or going of misfortune.

Reversed: Extravagance. Given to braggadocio. Tyranny over the helpless, be it man or animal. A person always ready to start a fight. Destruction may come about through the knight's activities.

KNIGHT of SWORDS.

QUEEN
OF SWORDS

On a high throne, looking into a clouded sky, sits a queen with a raised sword in her left hand. This suggests, "Let those approach who dare!" Her crown and the base of her throne are decorated with the butterflies of the soul, and just under the arm of the throne we find a sylph, the elemental of the air. The queen's face is chastened through suffering.

Choose this card for a brown-haired, brown-eyed woman.

Divinatory Meaning: A subtle, keen, and quick-witted woman who may represent a widow or one who is unable to bear children. Perhaps she is mourning for those she loves who are far away from her.

This card may mean widowhood, mourning, privation. Kindness but also firmness. Keen observation. Gracefulness; fondness for dancing.

Reversed: Unreliability. Narrow-mindedness. Gossip. Deceit. Malice. A woman of artifice and prudery.

QUEEN of SWORDS.

KING
OF SWORDS

A stern-looking king is seated on the throne of judgment. Behind him is a pillar (or tapestry) with a butterfly design, signifying the soul. (Swords are the symbol of the soul.) Behind him also we have the storm clouds and cypress trees that have appeared in each of the Court cards of the Swords. He represents law and order, the power of life and death.

Choose this card for a mature man with dark hair and eyes.

Divinatory Meaning: This is a man who may be a lawyer, a judge, a general, or a governor. He gives wise counsel, is firm in enmity as well as in friendship. A man of many ideas, thoughts, and designs.

The card may also mean power, strength, authority, or military intelligence. A lawsuit is in the offing.

Reversed: Distrustful, suspicious. Also harsh and malicious. Plotting, barbarity, power for disruption, are revealed.

KING of SWORDS.

The Pentacles

*ACE
OF
PENTACLES*

A hand comes forth from a cloud. This time it holds a golden pentacle. The lilies of pure thought grow in the garden below. The card represents Eternal Synthesis, the great whole of the visible universe, the realization of counterbalanced power.

Divinatory Meaning: The beginning of wealth and material gain. Gold, prosperity, combined with pleasure and beauty.

Reversed: Miserliness, greed. A false start. Comfortable material conditions, which may not be to the advantage of the Querent.

**TWO
OF
PENTACLES**

A young man in gay costume dances while he balances two pentacles held together by a cord shaped like a figure 8 on its side, the cosmic lemniscate of eternal life. The ships behind him are tossed on the high seas.

Divinatory Meaning: The ability to juggle two situations at one time. Lightheartedness, gaiety. Recreation. Harmony in the midst of change. New projects may be difficult to launch. News and messages in writing. A nature industrious yet unreliable, elated and then melancholic.

Reversed: Enforced gaiety; inability to handle several situations at once. Simulated enjoyment.

*THREE
OF
PENTACLES*

A nun and a monk watch a sculptor putting the finishing touches on a carving he is doing for the church. Three pentacles adorn the archway. See the sections on Numerology and the Kabalah, and note that three is the number of completion.

Divinatory Meaning: Material increase. The master craftsman, the skilled artist. Gain in a commercial transaction. This is the card for members of the Masons and other groups and societies.

Reversed: Lack of skill. Ignorance. Selfishness. Commonplace ideals; preoccupation with gain.

**FOUR
OF
PENTACLES**

Here is the miser clinging to his gold. He is hanging on tightly to his material possessions.

Divinatory Meaning: Assured material gain, success. Earthly power, but leading to nothing beyond it. Gifts, legacy, inheritance. May indicate a miserly, ungenerous character.

Reversed: Prejudice, covetousness, suspicion. Hindrances. Setbacks in material ambitions. The spendthrift, too free with money. Chance of loss of earthly possessions.

FIVE
OF
PENTACLES

A destitute man and woman pass under a lighted window. There is snow on the ground, and they appear to be in distress. In outer darkness, they have not yet realized the inner light.

Divinatory Meaning: Unemployment, destitution. Loss of home. Loneliness. Lovers unable to find a meeting place. Affinities discovered through similar troubles. Dark night of the soul.

Reversed: Money regained after severe toil. New employment, but this may not be permanent. Charity. A new interest in spiritual matters.

SIX
OF
PENTACLES

A good man, probably a merchant, gives money to the needy with balance and judgment. From a good heart, he shares with others.

Divinatory Meaning: Alms dispensed with justice; gifts, inheritance. Gain in material undertaking. Others will share with you justly. You will receive what you deserve.

Reversed: Purse-proud. Jealous. Bad debts. Present prosperity threatened. Gifts given, but as a bribe.

SEVEN
OF
PENTACLES

A strong young farmer leans on his hoe and gazes at the pentacles growing on the vine at his right. Will he receive the harvest from his work?

Divinatory Meaning: Pause during the development of an enterprise. Unprofitable speculations. Loss of promising fortune. Disappointment. Anxiety about a loan. Success not attained.

Reversed: Impatience. Little gain after much work. Again, anxiety about a loan.

EIGHT
OF
PENTACLES

The sculptor's apprentice is carving out a pentacle; he exhibits other pentacles on the post beside him. Compare this card with the Three of Pentacles, in which the sculptor has become a mature artist and receives his reward.

Divinatory Meaning: Learning a trade or profession. The beginning of a profitable undertaking. Employment or commission to come. Skill in material affairs, handiwork, and the arts—sometimes remaining only in the apprenticeship stage.

Reversed: There is danger of failing in one's ambitions. False vanity, intrigue, and sharp practice. Skill turned to cunning, like that of a counterfeiter.

**NINE
OF
PENTACLES**

A mature, well-dressed woman with a tame bird upon her wrist stands in her vineyard; there is a manor house in the background. She is alone, but she seems safe in her possessions. The bird, a falcon, represents well-controlled thought.

Divinatory Meaning: Solitary enjoyment of the good things of life. Inheritance. Wisdom where one's own interests lie. A person and a green thumb. Material well-being. Caution: be prudent. Great love of gardens and home.

Reversed: Danger from thieves, cancelled project. Possible loss of home or friendship. Move with caution.

TEN
OF
PENTACLES

A patriarch rests at ease before an archway on which is inscribed his coat of arms. His family and his dogs are with him, signifying the solidity of an ancient family carrying on in prosperity.

Divinatory Meaning: Riches, inheritance. Attention to family matters, interest in one's ancestral tree. A problem concerning a will or pension. May refer to the acquiring of a house or a business property.

Reversed: Family misfortune; old people may become a burden. Loss of inheritance. Caution against getting involved in projects that are a poor risk.

PAGE
OF PENTACLES

A prince or princess stands in a field and gazes at the pentacle that seems to float in the air before him. Although the Pentacles are the cards of money and earthly things, this Page is still a student, careful and diligent.

Choose this card for a boy or girl with black hair and eyes and a swarthy complexion.

Divinatory Meaning: Respect for learning and new ideas. A scholar. A typical introvert.

Can also mean application; reflection. Good management, carefulness. The bringer of good news and messages about money.

Reversed: Dissipation and excess. Too great pleasure in the material things of life. Wastefulness, luxury. News of the loss of money or wordly goods.

PAGE of PENTACLES.

KNIGHT
OF PENTACLES

This knight rides a heavy workhorse through a freshly plowed field. He wears a green sprig on his helment, and there is also a sprig in the horse's bridle. The knight is a materialist; he looks placidly at the symbol he carries.

Choose this card for a black-haired, black-with black hair, black eyes, and a swarthy skin.

Divinatory Meaning: A man of upright nature who accepts responsibility. He is laborious and patient.

The card can also mean utility, serviceableness, trustworthiness. Or the coming or going of an important matter connected with money.

Reversed: A static nature that is unprogressive, dull, timid, idle, or careless. It indicates stagnation in one's affairs.

KNIGHT of PENTACLES.

QUEEN
OF PENTACLES

Here is the Queen of Fertility seated on a throne with goat-head arms, ripe fruit, and a cupid at the back. She is surrounded by green fields, and the rabbit of fertility sits at her side nearby. A bower of red roses above her signifies desire. She sits quietly contemplating the pentacle she holds in her lap.

Choose this card to represent a woman with black hair and eyes.

Divinatory Meaning: This is a woman who is the Earth Mother, generous with her gifts. She is rich but charitable, a truly noble soul. A creator on the physical plane.

Other meanings are opulence; security. Trust of those around one. At times melancholy or moody. Good use of practical talents.

Reversed: Mistrust, suspicion. Duties neglected. Dependence on others. Changeable. Fearful of failure.

QUEEN of PENTACLES

KING
OF PENTACLES

The king holds a scepter to represent his power. In the other hand, he holds a pentacle. His robe is emblazoned with bunches of grapes and vine leaves; bulls' heads are depicted on the back and on the arms of his throne, and he is surrounded by flowers. His castle can be seen over his shoulder.

Choose this card for a black-haired, black-eyed man with swarthy skin.

Divinatory Meaning: This is a chief of industry, a banker, or owner of large estates. He is a reliable married man and a mathematician with great financial gifts.

The card can also betoken a steady temperament, slow to anger; success where money matters are concerned and reliability.

Reversed: Stupidity. Perverse use of talents. Thriftless. Easy to bribe. Vice. Caution against association with gamblers and speculators. If crossed, he could be a dangerous man.

KING of PENTACLES.

HOW TO READ
THE CARDS

Let us assume that you have a deck of Tarot cards, presumably the Rider Pack designed by A. E. Waite which is pictured in this book. After you have mastered the meanings of these cards, it will be relatively easy for you to use any of the decks now on the market, should you so desire.

HOW TO KEEP YOUR CARDS

It is wise to protect your Tarot deck not only from physical damage but also from discordant vibrations. Wrap your cards in a piece of silk (an old scarf will do). Silk is thought to be one of the best materials for keeping the pack isolated. Then put the wrapped cards in a small box—perhaps an attractive object in itself to have around. They should never be left scattered about; put them away when you have finished with them. When the cards are new, you might, as some people do, put them under your pillow for a few nights so that they can acquire your personal vibrations. Do this again if the cards have been left unused for a number of months or have been handled by a person whose presence has disturbed you.

HOW TO PREPARE YOURSELF

It is important that you study and really learn the meanings of each of the 78 cards. In some way that we do not understand, your subconscious mind seems to direct the shuffling but can do this correctly only after you have implanted the meaning of each card in your memory. Before you try to read for a friend, also familiarize yourself with the method of laying out the cards that you have decided to use. Half-learned meanings will result in half-correct answers.

Do not encourage levity in any of those present, for a reading is a serious attempt to go above the psychic realm to a higher level where Truth is accessible.

I would advise that you do not take the first few of your readings too seriously. In reading for yourself, be particularly careful that a happy mood does not incline you to over-rosy interpretations; likewise, if you are blue and discouraged, be sure to check how much your mood is affecting your reading.

SHUFFLING AND LAYING OUT THE CARDS

You have no doubt noticed the recurrent term "Reversed" under the "Divinatory Meanings" for each card. This, of course, means upside-down. A card in this position usually yields the opposite meaning to that of the card when right side up. If you are going to shuffle by riffling, then hold the cards so that the tops in each hand face each other. In this way they will be well mixed, with approximately half the cards facing in opposite directions. As they are shuffled again and again for each reading, they become very well mixed.

You are called the Reader, and the person for whom you are going to read is the Querent.

Before any shuffling is done, choose a Court card that corresponds to the age and coloring of the Querent. For example, choose a Page for boys under twenty-one and girls, too —unless they are married, in which case a Queen is chosen for them. Select a Knight for a young man; a King for a married, mature man; a Queen for any woman over twenty-one. Look up the descriptions of the Court cards and find one that is suitable. But do not, at this stage, attach too much importance to the card chosen. If the Querent feels she is the Queen of Wands in temperament, even though her hair is dark, it is quite all right. The Hierophant might be a good choice for a clergyman; the Emperor might be chosen for an important political figure. (Follow the directions given with the layout you have selected. It may direct you to put the Querent's card in the center of the spread or to place it back in the deck.)

It is best to have the Querent shuffle the deck, but if this seems impractical, the Reader may do so, asking the Querent to lay his hands on the deck before cutting it. While shuffling, the Querent should ask, silently, a simple but important question, repeating it over and over again mentally until he feels the question has entered the cards. It is best if the Reader does not know what the question is, since this knowledge might color his reading unduly. During the shuffling the Reader should silently ask that only the highest forces surround them. Later, when the reading is nearly finished, the question can be told and the cards then gone over for amplification.

After shuffling, the Querent cuts the cards into three piles, with the left hand toward the left, in true Gypsy fashion. The Reader then picks up the piles with the left hand, starting with the first pile put down.

THE LAYOUT

The cards from the top of the deck should be turned face up one by one and placed in an order corresponding to the diagram selected. When the requisite number of cards are laid out, the rest of the pack is put aside and not used.

Glance quickly at all the cards laid out, and note if there is a preponderance of any one suit or if there are many Court cards or cards of the Major Arcana. These will indicate a general trend or direction in the readings.

MANY WANDS — *Change*
MANY CUPS — *Love, goodness*
MANY SWORDS — *Strife*
MANY PENTACLES — *Political action or intrigue*

The presence of many of the Major Arcana indicates that the answer to the Querent's question is largely controlled by other people.

Remember that readings depend not only on the meaning of the individual card but also on its place in the layout, and that the cards on each side may also affect the interpretation.

Questions usually fall into one of the following categories:

1. LOVE, MARRIAGE, FAMILY SITUATIONS
2. MONEY, BUSINESS AFFAIRS, PROPERTY
3. PERSONAL ACCOMPLISHMENT, TRAVEL
4. STATES OF MIND; PROBLEMS ENCOUNTERED ON THE SPIR-
ITUAL PLANE

HOW TO INTERPRET THE CARDS

Try to make a running story about what you see in the cards
in relation to the person for whom you are reading. If you
have forgotten the meanings of some of the cards, look them
up—don't guess. (At the end of this chapter there is a list of
briefly summarized meanings for each card—if you need a
quick reminder.)

If, after reading the cards, the Querent tells you that his
question is not answered, ask him if the cards have perhaps
dealt with a deeper question that he has been worrying
about. I have found that people are sometimes a little timid
about bringing out into the open what is really on their
minds, and will ask a superficial question of the Tarot. With
a little digging and a sincere desire to help, you may uncover
what is really bothering the Querent and find that the cards
have indeed answered a question that really was uppermost
in his mind.

Perhaps you are psychic; the cards then will really come
alive for you and lead you right to the problem about which
the Querent needs to talk and get advice. Those who do not
feel that they are psychic will soon find, however, that they
are developing a sixth sense and that they intuitively feel
the inner implications of the situation.

Sometimes the cards do not seem to be responding at all.
In that case, ask the Querent to shuffle again and concentrate more deeply on the question. If, on reshuffling, the
cards still do not make sense, it would be well to put them
away for at least twenty-four hours before trying to read
them again.

NEVER, NEVER, NEVER finish the reading on a discouraging note. If the cards are bad, indicate how the
Querent can overcome the problems by work, study, application to tasks, better care of health, or by expending more

love and compassion in relationships. You may foretell—but only in a vague manner—the possible illness or death of someone the Querent knows, but *never predict a serious illness or death for the Querent*. Instead, say you see the possibility of a slight illness in the future, which could be avoided if the Querent would take better care of his health, and then quickly move on to interpreting a more positive section of the layout.

Reading the Tarot is a great responsibility. It gives you the opportunity to help others gain an insight into what may be holding them back from their fullest self-expression. Other people are as sensitive as you are, and giving a discouraging reading with no hope held out for the future is a cruel and pointless thing to do. Besides, we have all seen seemingly hopeless lives suddenly take remarkable turns for the better. While there is life, there is always hope.

So now you are on your own, to use your new skill with good taste and delicacy. For all its seriousness the Tarot can be fun—so enjoy it!

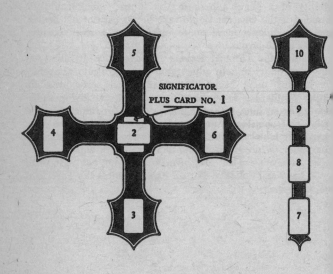

SIGNIFICATOR IS PLACED IN CENTER.

No. 1 THIS COVERS HIM.

No. 2 THIS CROSSES HIM.

No. 3 THIS IS BENEATH HIM.

No. 4 THIS IS BEHIND HIM.

No. 5 THIS CROWNS HIM.

No. 6 THIS IS BEFORE HIM.

No. 7 WHAT HE FEARS.

No. 8 FAMILY OPINION.

No. 9 HIS HOPES.

No. 10 FINAL OUTCOME.

Diagram 1. THE KELTIC METHOD

The Ancient Keltic Method

You, the Reader, have chosen a Court card to represent the Querent and have placed this in the middle of the table. The Querent has asked a question, either silently or aloud, and has thoroughly shuffled and cut the cards (to the left). Now you, the Reader, pick up the cards and lay out the top ten cards, face up, according to the diagram.

Read the meanings of each card in turn, in conjunction with the meanings ascribed to the number of the spot it is on.

1. THIS COVERS HIM. *The first card, in the center, represents the general atmosphere that surrounds the question asked and the influences at work around it.*

2. THIS CROSSES HIM. *This card should be laid across the first; it is always read right side up, and shows what the opposing forces may be for good or evil.*

3. THIS IS BENEATH HIM. *The basis of the matter—something that has already become part of the subject's experience in the past.*

4. THIS IS BEHIND HIM. *This shows the influence that is just passing away.*

5. THIS CROWNS HIM. *Represents something that may happen in the future.*

6. THIS IS BEFORE HIM. *Things that will come to pass in the near future—e.g., a meeting, an affair, a person, an influence.*

7. **WHAT THE QUERENT FEARS.** *The negative feelings he has about the question asked.*

8. **FAMILY OPINION.** *Represents Querent's environment, the opinions and influence of family and friends on the matter.*

9. **HOPES.** *Represents the Querent's own hopes and ideals in the matter.*

10. **FINAL OUTCOME.** *This tenth and last card tells what the final outcome will be. It should include all that has been divined from the other cards on the table.*

Now is the time to make a story out of your reading. Tell the Querent what you have seen in the cards about his past insofar as it concerns his question. Tell him what his future is likely to hold for him, the negative influences that he must watch out for, the good influences of which he must take advantage.

Should it happen that the last card is one from which no final conclusion can be drawn, it may be well to repeat the entire operation, putting the *tenth* card in place of the card originally chosen for the Querent. The pack should again be thoroughly shuffled as the Querent repeats his original question and asks for more clarification. Then the cards are cut and laid out as before. By this means, a more detailed account of the outcome may be obtained. If there is no satisfactory answer, the cards should be put away for that day, since it is evident that there is interference of some sort—or perhaps the answer to the question has not yet been resolved in the unseen.

A SAMPLE READING USING THE ANCIENT KELTIC METHOD

This is an actual reading I gave for a young girl named Jane, who had twice gotten into trouble with the law in connection with smoking marijuana. At the time of the reading she had been working for two months as a salesgirl in a department store, and was seemingly chastened by her brushes with the law.

Jane had chosen the Page of Cups to represent her, and had silently asked the question: "What will happen to me in the next six months?"

The first ten cards in the deck had been laid out, following the diagram, into the design of a cross and a staff. The first thing I did was to check whether there was a preponderance of the Major Arcana or of any one particular suit. The cards were exceptionally evenly divided—two Wands, two Swords, two Cups, two Pentacles, and two of the Major Arcana. I carefully studied each card and tried to relate it to the meaning of its location on the board.

Position 1: The Ten of Swords covered the Querent's card. This position indicates the atmosphere that surrounds the question. The meaning of the Ten of Swords here is ruin, pain, affliction, tears. This meaning certainly was true for the past, for Jane had been expelled from boarding school and later had been arrested while in college. She, as well as her family, had experienced pain and tears during these trying times.

Position 2: This is the card of the force opposing No. 1. Though this card is placed crosswise, it is always read as if it were right side up. In this instance, the card was the Ace of Cups. Aces always mean beginnings, and Cups would mean the beginnings of love and abundance. It would seem that in spite of recent troubles Jame could have a new and interesting life surrounded by love and abundance.

Position 3: Something that has already become part of Jane's experience. In this position was the Three of Pentacles, the card of the master craftsman. Jane was an excellent art student and at one time showed great promise as a painter.

Position 4: Here is the influence just passing away. The Knight of Swords was in this position, and it has many meanings. It can indicate an impetuous young man, but after consideration I chose the meanings of conflict and destruction, which, in this position, would indicate that they were going out of her life.

Position 5: This position shows the influence that may come into Jane's life in the future. Here was the Fool, a truly wonderful card, opening up all sorts of possibilities. Remembering the influence of the Ace of Cups, I felt that the choice the Fool indicated was whether to accept the new beginning or reject it.

Position 6: Shows the influence that will operate in the future. Here was the Two of Cups, also a card of new beginnings, perhaps a love affair, and surely a deep friendship with someone who would bring harmony into Jane's life.

Position 7: (the lowest card shown on the staff): This is the position of the Querent's fears. Here was the Ace of Wands, the beginning of an enterprise, or creation. At first this seemed contradictory, but perhaps Jane was afraid that if she attempted a creative enterprise she would fail. She might be timid about trying again and failing.

Position 8: This position indicates what others think of the Querent in relation to the question asked—in this case, Jane's family and friends. Justice, reversed, meaning legal complications and excessive severity, was in Position 8. Certainly lawyers had been required to keep Jane out of jail, and as she was still on probation at the time of the reading, she may have felt there was excessive severity in the restrictions imposed upon her.

Position 9: This position tells us about the Querent's hopes. The card here was the Five of Pentacles, and I interpreted it to mean that in spite of good prognostications for her future, Jane did not dare to put too much hope in them and still looked upon the next few months as a time of loneliness and material trouble.

Position 10: This is the final outcome—to which all the other cards have been leading. And here was the Nine of Wands, reversed, indicating obstacles and delay. These might possibly be the result of her negative attitude concerning her immediate future. The good cards in the layout were extremely good: two Aces showing new beginnings possible, a companion or sweetheart to plan and share with, and the Fool—a card of infinite possibilities.

My suggestions to Jane were to concentrate on the good aspects of the layout and to have more confidence in the good breaks that were coming her way. I advised her to be guided by the Fool, who cautions against unwise choices. On the whole, the Tarot seemed to suggest good possibilities for the future, but these would have to be grasped by Jane as she learned to be more optimistic and to choose the positive and constructive opportunities that presented themselves, rejecting the temptation to follow the destructive path she had taken in the past.

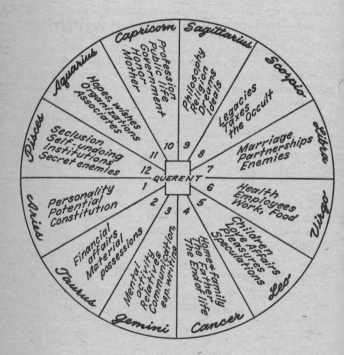

Diagram 2. THE HOROSCOPE METHOD

The Horoscope Method

This way of reading the Tarot will appeal to those who have made a study of Astrology, for they will find even more significant analogies than the average reader. But it will also be found to be a simple method for the person without such specialized knowledge.

The usual beginning steps are followed here: The Querent shuffles the cards and cuts them; then the Reader takes them up and lays the first card face up on the first House, the second card on the second House, and so on to the twelfth. Then a thirteenth card, that of the Querent, is laid in the middle of the circle to serve as the "Ruler" of the horoscope.

Each House is assigned to departments of life and given allotments of our earthly assets and experiences. These are listed here so that they can be referred to when interpreting the cards that have fallen to each House.

SOLAR HOUSE	RULER	MEANING IN DIVINATION
1.	ARIES	*Aries rules all beginnings, including childhood. It is assigned to the Querent's appearance and characteristics, also his worldly outlook and potential.*
2.	TAURUS	*This is the sign that conserves and builds. Concerns financial affairs and tangible assets.*
3.	GEMINI	*This is a mental sign that links people together through like thought. It is assigned to relatives, neighbors; also to communications: letters, roads, writings, and short journeys.*

4.	CANCER	*The fourth House begins at the point of midnight; therefore it is assigned to all endings. Old age, old people, parents, and the home environment.*
5.	LEO	*This is the natural House of Leo, which governs the heart. Love affairs, children, things that cause excitement: theatres, gambling, speculations.*
6.	VIRGO	*This House rules work, employees, food, hygiene, and general health of the Querent.*
7.	LIBRA	*This House rules both marriage and business partners, dealings with the public, lawsuits, open enemies.*
8.	SCORPIO	*Rules death, legacies, insurance policies; also the partner's money. Sex. Occult experiences.*
9.	SAGITTARIUS	*Rules law, philosophy, and religion. Also dreams, psychic experiences, long journeys, and foreign countries.*
10.	CAPRICORN	*Profession, promotion, fame. Also parentage and social status. Concerns government.*
11.	AQUARIUS	*This House rules the friends you have made; groups, clubs to which you belong. It has some rule over the money you earn from your profession, financial conditions of employer. Hopes, wishes, aspirations.*
12.	PISCES	*Hidden limitations that restrict your power of expression. Secrets, secret enemies, self-undoing. This House also rules institutions; the basic strength or weakness of Querent's body and soul.*

As an example, let us say that the Two of Cups in a layout falls on Leo in the fifth House, which governs the heart and love. The Two of Cups can mean either a love affair or a new friendship. In this case, it should be read as a love affair. If it fell on Aquarius in the eleventh House, however, it could well mean a new friendship, perhaps made through a club or organization, since the eleventh House means both friendship and matters that concern organization.

Another example: If the Nine of Swords, reversed—meaning imprisonment, suspicion, and shame—fell on the twelfth House, Pisces, it could well mean that the Querent had either been in prison or might go there shortly. If it fell on the first House, Aries, which rules beginnings and childhood, it might indicate a parent who had been in prison or in some way brought shame on the Querent.

A SAMPLE READING BY THE HOROSCOPE METHOD

(If you pick out the twelve Tarot cards mentioned in this reading and lay them out in a large circle in their proper order, it will be easier for you to follow this reading.)

Arthur B., a college professor, was visiting in the East this past summer and one evening came to see us. When he found I was writing a new book on the Tarot, he asked me if I would read his cards. He was transferring from a college in the South to one on the West Coast, and was anxious to know how things would go for him during the coming academic year.

We decided on the horoscope spread and chose the King of Cups to represent him, putting it in the middle of the table. After he had shuffled and cut the cards, I took the top twelve cards from the pack and laid them in a circle—putting the first card on Aries, the second on Taurus, and so forth. Here are the cards that came up:

ARIES	*King of Swords*
TAURUS	*Eight of Swords*
GEMINI	*The Hanged Man*
CANCER	*Strength, Reversed*
LEO	*Knight of Swords*
VIRGO	*Seven of Swords, Reversed*
LIBRA	*Page of Cups*
SCORPIO	*Five of Wands*
SAGITTARIUS	*Three of Cups, Reversed*

CAPRICORN   *Knight of Cups*
AQUARIUS   *Five of Pentacles, Reversed*
PISCES   *Seven of Pentacles, Reversed*

In the first House, Aries, that of the personality, self-interest, and worldly outlook generally, we had the King of Swords. Since this is the House of the Querent's personality and he was not the type to fit the description of the King of Swords, it was interpreted that inwardly he would very much like to have that kind of personality and "be a wise man, a counsellor full of helpful ideas."

In the second House, Taurus, that of financial affairs, we had the Eight of Swords. Here the figure of the woman bound and surrounded by Swords seemed to indicate that Arthur's financial affairs were somewhat straitened. He had been getting a good salary at his former post and was to get an even better one at the college he was going to, but perhaps he had made some unfortunate speculation that was now embarrassing him.

In the third House, Gemini, that of the intellect and communication, was the Hanged Man. Though this can be a spiritual card, Arthur's question was on a practical level, and so the card was taken to indicate that there would be an interruption in his intellectual or writing pursuits. A heavy work load of teaching, in addition to some anxiety as to how he would fit into a Western college, might cause him to put off any outside, creative efforts.

In the fourth House, Cancer, that of home environment, domestic affairs, parentage, state of things at the close of life, we had Key 8, Strength, reversed. As Arthur is a bachelor and has no present domestic life, the card seemed to indicate that as a child the emphasis in his home had been on the material things and that he himself would be materially inclined well into his later years.

In the fifth House, Leo, that of love affairs, pleasurable emotions arising from the senses and speculations, the card was the Knight of Swords—a dark-haired young man, strong and domineering. I felt this Knight had already come into Arthur's life and that there was some sort of emotional attachment. Since this is also the House of speculation, through the friend's domination Arthur had been led to make an investment of a speculative nature that kept him financially bound.

In the sixth House, Virgo, that of matters of health, employees, work and food, was the Seven of Swords, reversed. This was the fourth Sword in the spread, and as many Swords as that surely mean trouble of some sort. Here, however, the card was in its reversed position so that it meant good advice and counsel would be given by Arthur to those who worked under him, and he, in turn, would also be helped in arranging his teaching assignments.

In the eighth House, Scorpio, we find things concerning legacies, taxes, death, and astral experiences. The card was the Five of Wands. It is always up to the Reader to determine how he will combine the meaning of the card with its zodiacal sign so that they fit as a pair and blend into the meaning of the reading as a whole. This card could mean many things, but it had to be fitted into the meanings of Scorpio in this instance. I adjudged that the death of a relative would bring Arthur a legacy, but that there would be some litigation before he got the money.

In the ninth House, Sagittarius, we find long journeys, religion, idealism, philosophy, and higher education. The card—the Three of Cups, reversed—indicated an excess of physical enjoyment. In some way, Arthur had perverted his philosophy and his idealism to fit in with his sensual physical nature and his love of fine food and material possessions.

In the tenth House, Capricorn, are profession, acclaim, ambition, promotion. The card here was the Knight of Cups, probably a younger colleague who would help Arthur advance to a position of prominence in the teaching field.

In the eleventh House, Aquarius, that of friends, hopes, and wishes, was the Five of Pentacles, reversed. In this position it has the meaning of good companionship—especially when coupled with Aquarius.

In the twelfth House, Pisces, we have unexpected troubles, limitations, self-undoing, and secret enemies. The card was the Seven of Pentacles, reversed, meaning cause for anxiety over money, impatience. Thus, again we had the trouble about money coming up, and I warned Arthur not to be too uneasy if he had loaned money to a friend or made a bad investment.

The overall horoscope reading for Arthur seemed to indicate that he would meet with friends and promotion in his new professorial position. The Knight of Swords that was in the fifth House, Leo, might be the one who entangled him in some financial matter that would turn out badly, and that he was brooding about. The general outlook, however, was a good one, the cards predicting success for the coming year.

THE EGYPTIAN TAROT. *These cards are now produced by The Church of Light, California, and used by C. C. Zain in* Sacred Tarot. *The Fool, here a youth, carries two bags on his staff; a crocodilian rests on a broken obelisk. (This card is numbered 22.) In the Tower the figures fall from a pyramid. The Hanged Man remains much the same, though Egyptianized. The King of Cups holds a cup in one hand and a heart in the other.*

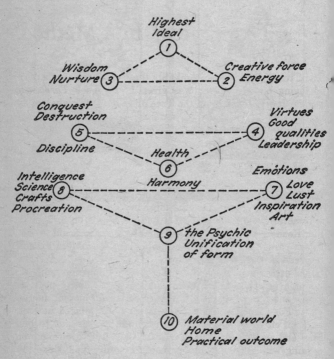

Diagram 3. THE TREE OF LIFE METHOD

The Tree of Life Method

The Tree of Life spread, probably the most complete method of laying out the cards, was given in my book *Tarot Revealed*. It was taken from the Tree of Life of the Kabalah, as can be seen by comparing Diagram 3 with Diagram 4 in the section on The Tarot and the Kabalah. We divide the Tree into three triangles, the first one pointing up, indicating its spiritual and mental nature; the second and third point downward to more material aspects. We also must keep in mind the three pillars or branches. A card placed on the right-hand branch must be read with mercy and compassion, whereas a card falling on the left-hand branch is to be read with severity. For instance, if a bad card falls on 3, 5, or 8, the Reader should be critical—perhaps even scold a bit. Those cards that fall on the numbers of the middle branch are read in a spirit of harmony.

(A person experienced in the art of divination may attempt a complete Life reading by using the entire pack of cards and leaving the card chosen for the Querent in the pack. For this Life reading, seven cards are placed at each number on the Tree, with the remaining cards put to one side and called the Daath Pack. An entire afternoon or evening will be needed for a reading of this type, since the cards are spread out three times—once for the past, once for the present, and the third time for the future. A complete Tree of Life reading should not be done for any Querent oftener than once a year.)

DIRECTIONS FOR LAYING OUT CARDS

Choose a Court card to represent the Querent. This card may be put to one side or it may be replaced in the deck. If it is

167

put back into the deck and should turn up in the spread, the indication would be to look with special attention at that particular number of the Tree and its meaning in relation to the Querent.

The Querent shuffles the deck, as usual, silently asking a question; then the cards are cut and laid out in the three triangles, with No. 10 as the trunk of the tree. Then count out the next seven cards and put them aside. This is the Daath Pack, which should be turned up and read only after the rest of the reading is completed.

CARD 1—The Querent's highest ideals
CARD 2—His creative power. The   *Triangle 1*
        "father" card   Spirituality
CARD 3—His wisdom. Ability to   Highest ideals
        bring ideas into form

CARD 4—Virtues, good qualities,
        ability to build up   *Triangle 2*
CARD 5—Force, conquest, tendency   Intellectual and
        to destruction   moral nature of
CARD 6—Health, beauty, tendency to   Querent
        sacrifice for others

CARD 7—Love, instincts, arts, lust
CARD 8—Procreation, crafts, science,   *Triangle 3*
        design   Desires. Ability to
CARD 9—Imagination, psychic senses,   direct and control
        engineering

CARD 10—The Querent's physical body
        or earthly home

A SAMPLE READING BY THE
TREE OF LIFE METHOD

This reading was chosen for two reasons: first, it was made over a year ago and we can therefore judge whether the cards divined correctly; second, the Querent, Patricia, is in her middle thirties and married, in contrast to our first reading of a teen-ager and the second of a bachelor.

Patricia is tall, dark, and stunning, rather than pretty, and though she took most things with a laugh, one could sense a sadness or melancholy underneath. We met at a party, and the next day she phoned and begged for a reading. She had a problem, she said, and was sure the Tarot could help her.

We used the Tree of Life layout, and I asked Patricia not to tell me her question but to ask it silently as she shuffled the cards. The Queen of Swords was chosen to represent the Querent, and laid to one side.

1. Temperance
2. Five of Swords
3. Four of Pentacles, reversed
4. Queen of Wands, reversed
5. The Tower
6. The Moon
7. King of Cups
8. Three of Pentacles, reversed
9. Two of Cups, reversed
10. The Star

   (The Daath Pack of seven cards is used to qualify and enlarge upon the above cards. The Daath cards are laid out in a row and read from right to left. Here we had: King of Swords; Six of Swords; Ten of Wands; Strength; Two of Swords, reversed; Ace of Cups; Two of Wands.)

No. 1: Temperance, at the top of the Tree of Life, the place of one's highest ideals, indicated that Patricia wanted to be the one who creates and, in a sense, to choose and dominate those around her. She has a keen, quick wit (Queen of Swords) and used this to help her create the kind of world she wanted.

2: "The Five of Swords here means that managing the lives of those about you may be an empty victory; you are possibly causing discontent," I told Patricia.

3: "The Four of Pentacles, reversed. This falls on the place of wisdom and the creative force of the mother. There are setbacks in your material aspirations. You have tried to force things by spending more money than you should, possibly to further your plans to make others follow your will."

4: "Here is the place of good qualities, a building-up force. But, contradicting this, we have the Queen of Wands, reversed, a blonde, blue-eyed woman who is in opposition to you. There is deceit and jealousy."

Patricia nodded, "Yes, I know about her; she works in my husband's office."

5: "Here is the breaking-down force of Geburah, and the card is the Tower on the pillar of severity, so I must tell you bluntly what I see. The Tower indicates a change in your way of life. From now on Spirit will illumine your path. Your present way of running things and ruining them is over. There is a chance that this blonde woman will cause your husband to leave you."

6: "This is the place of the Sun that draws all other vibrations to it; here we also have health and perhaps sacrifice. The card is the Moon, which can mean the unfoldment of latent powers of intuition." I asked Patricia if she was inclined to be psychic, and she said she thought she was—a little. "Use this faculty, then, to understand what the cards are trying to say to you; use your intuition and imagination; correct the picture of the cards above, and you will be able to avoid much trouble."

7: "The King of Cups here has fallen on the place of love, lust, and the arts. Could this card be your husband?"

"Yes, I think it is. He is an art director in an advertising agency in New York."

"I feel," I said to her, "that he is basically a very kind and generous man, as well as quite talented."

8: "The Three of Pentacles, reversed, falls here on the place of the intellect, design, crafts, and procreation. The Three of Pentacles is the card of the master craftsman, but here it is reversed, meaning he is not giving his best to his job; his work is mediocre—he could do much better. The pull on his affections between you and the Queen of Wands is tearing him apart."

9: "At No. 9, the meanings of all the other cards are gathered together, and then we see what the final outcome will most probably be. Here we have the Two of Cups, reversed, which indicates a possible breaking up of a partnership. It could mean the breaking up of your marriage, or your husband's being fired from his job—or it could mean both. It is up to you to use your latent intuitive faculties and change your ways, and you may be able to bring your marriage back from the brink of destruction. Your attitude has been a very materialistic one, and to please you your husband may have sacrificed artistic integrity to gain your approval."

10: "This is the final place on the Tree. It represents the physical body and earthly home. The card here is the Star, one of hope and courage. Perhaps a little spiritual application would be good—prayer and meditation on the true meaning of Life. I feel you will be helped—if you are sincere and see your husband as more than just a provider. He is the King of Cups, you know, and therefore emotional. Love, tenderness, and caring mean a great deal to him. Take this card, the Star, into meditation, as suggested in the chapter on meditation, and there can definitely be a change for the better."

In the Daath or qualifying pack, we found the following:

1. The King of Swords. "He is perhaps an old family friend, a lawyer, someone you can trust, who can give you helpful ideas, which could bring you and your husband together again."

2. Six of Swords. "This card can indicate a trip, but in your case I feel it is more of a journey in consciousness for you. The family friend could be sent to plead your case."

3. Ten of Wands. "There will be a difficult period of waiting, but I must warn you not to threaten. Have you a child?" I asked.

"Yes, a little girl eight years old."

"Well, don't punish your husband by not letting him see her as often as he wishes."

4. Strength. "Here you are being shown the way. By trusting your higher nature and learning that spiritual power overcomes the material, you can have the satisfaction of seeing spiritual love overcome indifference."

5. Two of Swords, reversed. "If you will profit by this Tarot reading, there will be a release of the present situation and things will begin to move toward a reunion—but you must go slowly."

6. Ace of Cups. "This is a very good card that means an abundance of love and joy through the nourishment of spiritual sources. The card is saying that you and your husband can be together again. It is also a card of fertility, so don't be too surprised if you have another child."

7. Two of Wands. "You, like the merchant in the card,

have done all you can. Now is the time to wait gracefully, meditate creatively, so that this situation can work out to the best interests of all."

Patricia was obviously somewhat shaken by my reading and left rather hurriedly. It was at least a year before I met her again, at an art exhibition. She left her friends and came over to greet me with a warm smile. "Everything's all right," she whispered. "My husband and I are back together again. And the cards were right—I am going to have another baby."

DEFINITIONS SUMMARIZED

For convenient reference in divination, the following are brief descriptions of each of the cards:

Major Arcana

0	THE FOOL	*A choice is offered*
1	THE MAGICIAN	*Creative power*
2	THE HIGH PRIESTESS	*Hidden influences*
3	THE EMPRESS	*Material abundance, fertility*
4	THE EMPEROR	*Leadership*
5	THE HIEROPHANT	*Rule by the conventional*
6	THE LOVERS	*Choice between two loves*
7	THE CHARIOT	*Conquest of mind over emotions*
8	STRENGTH	*Triumph of love over hate*
9	THE HERMIT	*Wisdom offered*
10	THE WHEEL OF FORTUNE	*Ups and downs of life, good luck*
11	JUSTICE	*Balance, legal matters*
12	THE HANGED MAN	*Self-surrender to higher wisdom*
13	DEATH	*Change, renewal*
14	TEMPERANCE	*Adaptation, coordination*
15	THE DEVIL	*Temptation, bondage to the material*
16	THE TOWER	*Overthrow of selfish ambition*
17	THE STAR	*Health, hope, inspiration*
18	THE MOON	*Deception, unforeseen perils*
19	THE SUN	*Attainment, liberation, marriage*
20	JUDGMENT	*Spiritual awakening*
21	THE WORLD	*Triumph in all undertakings*

Minor Arcana

WANDS

ACE	*Beginning of fortune or family*
TWO	*Success in business*
THREE	*A partnership, help offered*
FOUR	*Romance, harvest, home*
FIVE	*Struggle, competition*
SIX	*Success, good news*
SEVEN	*Courage in difficult situations*
EIGHT	*Swift action, journey, message*
NINE	*Strength to overcome trouble*
TEN	*Heart tried by pain*
PAGE	*A young lover, a messenger*
KNIGHT	*Impetuous young man. Journey by water, the coming or going of a matter*
QUEEN	*A blond woman who is both home- and nature-loving* *Honest and practical*
KING	*Blond married man of authority. Devoted friend*

CUPS

ACE	*Beginning of love, joy, fertility*
TWO	*Love affair, deep friendship*
THREE	*Health, abundance*
FOUR	*Discontent, reevaluation*
FIVE	*Regret, rejection of pleasure*
SIX	*Happy memories*
SEVEN	*Castles in the air*
EIGHT	*Abandoning present situation*
NINE	*Material wealth (the wish card)*
TEN	*Happy family life*
PAGE	*Captivating boy or girl. Studious, friendly*
KNIGHT	*A romantic young man. He brings proposals and invitations*
QUEEN	*A romantic woman with intuition. A good wife and mother*
KING	*A reliable man of business, law, or divinity*

SWORDS

ACE	*Conquest, victory*
TWO	*Balanced forces, indecision*

THREE	*Sorrow, separation*
FOUR	*Solitude, change for the better*
FIVE	*An empty victory*
SIX	*Journey by water; difficulties fade away*
SEVEN	*A plan may fail*
EIGHT	*Bondage, restricted surroundings*
NINE	*Desolation, sorrow over another*
TEN	*Misfortune, pain, ruin*
PAGE	*An active young man or girl. Upsetting message*
KNIGHT	*Chivalrous young man, quick to defend or fight. Coming or going of a matter*
QUEEN	*A dark woman of strong character, acquainted with fortune*
KING	*A dark man with military or civilian authority*

PENTACLES

ACE	*Beginning of prosperity, wealth*
TWO	*Handling two situations at once*
THREE	*The master craftsman; skill in arts and sciences*
FOUR	*Legacy; material possessions held tightly*
FIVE	*Loneliness, destitution*
SIX	*Charity, gifts justly given*
SEVEN	*A pause during growth*
EIGHT	*Apprenticeship, small skills, employment to come*
NINE	*Solitary enjoyment of wealth*
TEN	*Established family of wealth, inheritance*
PAGE	*Studious youth or girl. Favorable news*
KNIGHT	*Dark, methodical young man, patient and responsible*
QUEEN	*A dark woman with black eyes, intelligent and thoughtful, lavish with her wealth*
KING	*A chief of industry; mathematical gifts; generosity, affection*

6

THE TAROT AND MEDITATION

The purpose of meditation is to reopen the spiritual pathway between man and the Infinite Intelligence, and thus to create within man's own soul a center for the activity of higher degrees of consciousness. Ignorance, discord, and fear are the barriers that obstruct access to this inner resource. To learn the truth about our relationship to the Infinite Intelligence is to be set free to enjoy the rewarding experience of traversing that pathway at will.

The most important reason for the use of the Will is to keep the mind stayed on higher things. We commonly think of Will as that power we use when making a choice between alternatives, but in reality we unconsciously choose the one that previous experience tells us is the more attractive. When the Spiritual Will is hampered in its operation, the emotions are likely to take over and we are said to lack self-control.

It is obvious enough that when one is in the grip of uncontrollable rage, the emotions are out of control. And, at the other extreme, one's emotions may be deeply repressed—perhaps because of the fear that they may become unmanageable if expressed. Not so obvious, however, is the loss of control of the mind. In that case, the mind throws out all data that do not conform to its preconceptions. This is the state of many "confirmed agnostics," who are no

175

more to be admired for their "intellectual honesty" than those at the opposite pole—the evangelists who express religious frenzy arising from emotional frustration.

The aim of the practicing occultist is to be able to discipline the mind and to use it, rather than to be used by it. The imagination must also be kept in control, for when it is permitted to run riot, even in so minor a matter as anticipation of a session with the dentist, it creates disproportionate apprehension.

The basic factor in achieving power over the mind is learning to control the attention—to focus awareness on a small area of thought. This ability to concentrate is, in fact, a necessary component for success in any undertaking. Voluntary attention is achieved by an act of the Will. When there is a strong sense of purpose in a given direction, our interest and attention move toward it. Continual practice in holding the attention pinpointed on one subject enhances our powers of concentration.

By means of the Will, the Spirit can make itself felt on earth, for nothing can stand against a firmly based and dedicated Will. Think of the many Christian martyrs who held to their beliefs through the most excruciating torture. And of Gandhi who, through the Will of the Spirit, held fast till India was free of English rule.

The student of the Tarot and the Kabalah—both forms of Western occultism—finds it profitable to spend time meditating on the Tree of Life and its related Tarot symbols. First, it is necessary to have imprinted strongly and deeply in the subconscious mind the structure of the Tree of Life and its attributions.

Occult teachers warn that casually undertaken psychic work tends to be fraught with illusions, useless diversions, and dead ends. Therefore, unless one has built up an understanding of cosmic symbolism such as that of the Tree of Life, it is better to leave meditation alone.

Another warning to the uninitiated: never open yourself to meditation in a passive or negative mood. Automatic writing, for example, is dangerous, since it is accomplished by making yourself passive to the very forces and powers toward which you should be positive and against which you should stand steadfast as a rock. It is a risky practice to empty yourself mentally and allow just anything to enter—this must be firmly avoided.

Now that you have been forewarned, here are some of the benefits that can accrue from meditation. By keeping ourselves in tune with our own inner Spirit we increase the flow of vital Life-force to every part of both mind and body, and we find we can accomplish the tasks of the day with greater ease. Meditation can become a joyous ritual, a time for spiritual refreshment, a time to realign and reclassify experiences according to inner knowing instead of outer appearance. The Fool's journey through the trials of learning can now be seen as relevant to our present movement, and the eternal values thus brought to our attention give courage as we progress along the way. This all takes place as the barriers to the upper reaches of mind are gradually broken down and intuition becomes linked with and available to normal consciousness.

Meditation requires its own place and time—a quiet room where no one will disturb you; a set time each day—the subconscious is a creature of habit. It is not a good idea to meditate while lying on a couch or bed, for if you are too comfortable you are likely to fall asleep, and meditation requires inward alertness.

In training the attention to follow consciously a single train of thought, one specific Tarot card should be chosen and its symbols and their meanings gone over in your mind. When reason has done its best in explaining the symbols, slowly relax through measured breathing and say, "I now release from my conscious mind the knowledge I have of this Tarot card, and I rise into the realm of all wisdom and ask to be shown its inner meanings." Then sit quietly and prepare to become a channel for cosmic wisdom.

The subconscious thinks in pictures and symbols. Thus, by taking a Tarot card into meditation, you have before you a picture that is filled with universal symbols. The deep unconscious is already familiar with these, and with prompting, it will bring them to the surface mind once again. Symbols act as mental footholds so that thoughts can pass logically and unfaltering from a symbol to an eternal principle, and by being aware of the relationship of symbol to principle, we develop understanding.

Meditation is not an experience given exclusively to devotees of religion or the occult—it is a normal, conscious process for self-development. But it must be earned through attention, concentration, and a willingness to be silent and to let ideas come through the superconscious by way of inspiration. Steadfast, persistent endeavor in meditation techniques, even through a hundred failures, is the dedication of the mystic and the occultist.

Thoughts are realities, and cosmic thoughts translate themselves into harmonious life. Friends, home, all material things, respond to the law of vibration and reflect the inner harmony that is made to shine upon them.

THE HIGH PRIESTESS AS AN EXAMPLE

Choose any card to meditate on that appeals to you, and when you have explored most of its possibilities, go on to the next one. I have chosen the High Priestess to use as an example—but not because this card is any better for meditation than any one of the others.

The High Priestess represents the subconscious mind, the instincts, emotions, memories—not only those of our own personal past but those of all mankind. The subconscious is also our link with the superconscious, our Divine Self, as brought out in Key 6, the Lovers. There we have the man representing the conscious mind looking to the woman, the subconscious, and she looks at the angel, the superconscious. We cannot bypass the subconscious in our search for the Divine within, and it is a good subject for our meditations.

The High Priestess sits between two pillars and is the balance between the positive and negative forces. The evil behind her has both male and female symbols on it—again balance. The Solar Cross at her breast repeating the same idea, for the positive (male) force in the vertical line, is equal to the negative (female) force of the horizontal line. Both are needed; both are equally important. In Diagram 4 of the Tree of Life, the fourth Sephiroth, Chesed, which builds up, is equally balanced with No. 5, Geburah, the force that breaks down. Do you see these two forces at work in the world around you? Do you see that both are necessary?

The Tree is divided into three pillars: the one on the left, Severity; on the right, Mercy; and between them the pillar of Harmony, the control between the two opposing forces. The High Priestess sits between a different version of these pillars, but her place in the middle is again that of harmony. The half-hidden scroll suggests the vast store of knowledge that is protected from those who do not approach the mysteries of life with the reverence that is their due.

These symbols can be a means of support to the mind as it advances through unknown and untried ways. They afford connecting links of thought that can carry the mind, without a break, from details to general principles. It is said that the subconscious mind cannot accept an absolutely new idea but must always relate new knowledge to something it has grasped before. Symbols, pictures, and diagrams give it a known concept to hang onto as thought proceeds from that which is understood into the vast unknown.

Using the Will to keep our minds centered on things of the Spirit—rather than on pushing or battling our way through the world—we begin, more and more, to achieve a charmed life. Our good flows to us through unexpected channels.

Through meditating on the Tarot, we begin to understand the evolution of Life and the Intelligence behind all manifestation, which we call God. We learn that on the physical plane there must be the tearing-down force (Geburah) as well as the building-up force (Chesed); that they must balance—not too much of any one species, or an opposing species will arrive to bring equilibrium. We see death as the necessary opposite of life, and God in each atom, each particle—the Life-force that never dies but reappears again and again, ever renewed, with its own inexhaustible Cosmic Energy.

We learn that to be an occultist is to be a "little god" with minor powers of creation. We can speak our word and it is done—as long as we have first acquired the knowledge of the workings of the Law of Cause and Effect, and work along with it.

The occultist never violates the laws of the universe but has learned to use them on a higher plane to create for himself the surroundings of his choice. He becomes the central Pillar of the Tree of Life, balancing the positive and negative elements, like the child in Key 20, the Sun, who rides forth at last from the walled garden of the cramped city of duality behind him, into the open and unexplored country of his own superconsciousness.

SYSTEMS OF OCCULT THOUGHT THAT ILLUMINATE THE TAROT

The three sections that follow discuss the relation between the Tarot and Numerology, the Kabalah, and Astrology, respectively. They are presented for those who may wish to go more deeply into the underlying harmonies that exist in all realms of metaphysics. At times the connections may be a little blurred, and the occultist may seem to be straining to fit them into his own theories, but the correspondences are too many to dismiss lightly.

An understanding of these related disciplines will surely reward the seeker after knowledge of the Tarot. The point is that no one can confine a philosophy as potent as the Tarot to the straitjacket of rigid dogma, and that we should extract from all these storehouses perceptions that will enrich and expand insight into the mystic cards. Today, when the interest in all esoteric and metaphysical realms of thought is at an unparalleled peak of intensity, the attempt to reach a basic core of meaning that unites them—each enhancing the others—is an exhilarating experience. I hope that my readers will find it so.

The Tarot and Numerology

"The world is built upon the power of numbers."
—Pythagoras

"Every cosmogony is based upon, interlinked with and
most closely related to numerals and geometrical figures."
—H. P. Blavatsky

In studying the origin of numbers, we come upon the opinion that the Hindus, from whom Pythagoras is said to have gained his knowledge of numbers, considered them a sacred science of the priesthood, and that the priests themselves declared numbers to be a direct revelation of the gods.

The Hebrews also attached significance to numbers, relating them to cosmic forces. They did not use separate systems of letters and numbers, but their letters were actually based upon numbers. They were placed in an order and given a form that would suggest the successive levels in the process of cosmic evolution. In both the Greek and Hebrew names in the Bible there is evidence of a very close relationship between literal and numerical meanings.

In the original Greek, "Jesus" is "Iesous" (there is no "J" in the Greek alphabet). This name is the numerical equivalent of 888, which, to initiates, represents the "Higher Mind" or "Divine Mind" in the Greek Mysteries. "Mortal Mind" in Greek is the number 666 (referred to in Revelation as the "beast").

Thus, there is a universal language that speaks to us through numbers. The key to it is symbolism, the inner sense of which remains unchanged throughout human history.

Numbers, as used in Numerology, are based on tens, the number 10 closing the first cycle, number 20 the second, and

so forth. There are 9 digits and hence 9 root influences, but
there are 10 separate characters. The universally accepted
method of reducing the letters of the alphabet to numerical
quantities, generally referred to as the "Pythagorean"
method, is very closely allied to the older Greek, Roman,
and Hebrew methods, and has been adapted to the English
alphabet.

The numerical designations follow the order of the alphabet. The letters and their corresponding numerical values
are indicated in the following table:

1	2	3	4	5	6	7	8	9
a	b	c	d	e	f	g	h	i
j	k	l	m	n	o	p	q	r
s	t	u	v	w	x	y	z	

It can be seen that the letter "O" the fifteenth letter of
the alphabet, is given the value of 6 in the table. The reason
for this is that the digits of 15 equal 6 $(1 + 5 = 6)$. All
double numbers are similarly reduced by being added into
a single number.

The above list holds good for simple Numerology, but the
Tarot Keys that are numbered above 9 embody both the
meanings of their sequential number and the aggregate of
their digits. For example, the Number 15 for the Devil,
like 15 in the consecutive numbers, relates to eroticism.
When the digits 1 and 5 are added together, making 6,
this relates the Devil to Key 6, the Lovers. In the first instance, the suggestion is thought and action brought down
to their lowest level; in the second instance we see thought
lifted to the plane of the superconscious.

The decimal system was held sacred by the Egyptian
priesthood, who declared they had received it directly from
the Divine teachers of mankind. The whole evolution of the
Cosmos and of man was said to be portrayed in the numbers
from 1 to 10, but it was revealed only to those who had
eyes to see. Number 10, being the sacred number of the
universe, was secret—a system of counting by 125 was re-
served for the common man.

NUMBERS AND THE TAROT CARDS

As we know, there are 22 cards in the Major Arcana,

numbered from 1 to 21 plus the 0. Many interpreters have tried to match these numbered cards with the 22 letters of the Hebrew alphabet. (This will be gone into more thoroughly in the section on the Tarot and the Kabalah.)

Here we will compare the meanings of the cards with the meanings of the numbers. In most instances, there seems to be a direct connection, but we also find cards whose meanings do not coincide with the meanings of their respective numbers. Of course, this discrepancy may be due to the fact that we no longer know the original arrangement of the Keys in the Major Arcana and can only approximate their proper numerical order. But, as we have said, the Tarot also stands alone, and although it is related to Numerology, Astrology, and the Kabalah, it is not a direct descendant of any one of them.

The *Number 0* is the first symbol to be considered, since all others proceed from it. It is related to Unmanifest Deity, a boundless circle of the pulsating, vibrant, yet undifferentiated Life-force having neither beginning nor end. It represents boundless space and limitless time in eternity. In the Tarot, Key 0, the Fool, carries out this significance.

Number 1 represents the principle of unity that underlies all numbers; it is the first manifestation of the unmanifest. It is the active principle that, broken into fragments, gives rise to multiplicity. By multiplication it creates all others, but multiplied by itself to infinity it always retains its unity. Number 1 is equated with the One God; the oneness of mankind; the power of Selfhood; of self-reliance, dignity, rulership. It is the Wand of the Magician, the power placed in Man's hands to accomplish through Will. Therefore, we can easily see how Number 1 relates to Tarot Key 1, the Magician.

Number 2 is the symbol of duality, the Mother-principle, as separate from the Father-principle of Number 1, which is now broken up into its positive and negative elements. Number 2 signifies a pair of opposites: good and evil, truth and error, day and night, heat and cold, joy and sorrow, male and female. In the Tarot, Key 2, the High Priestess, expresses much the same meaning.

Number 3 is the number of trinity—father, mother, and son. It also symbolizes the balance of all manifested things, the magnetic force of Divine Love permeating humanity. It is the vibratory effect of the interaction of Numbers 1 and 2, the fruit of their union—the son, or the material universe in all its fecundity. Thus the meaning of Tarot Key 3, the Empress, parallels that in numerology.

Number 4 is the number of the physical plane. The geometrical figure corresponding to 4 is the square, the base of the pyramid, the most stable of all forms. The various forms of the cross symbolize 4 because Spirit, represented by the vertical line when penetrating matter (the horizontal line), forms a cross with equal arms. This number also indicates that labor has reached completion—the fruit of the toil or union indicated in Number 3. Tarot Key 4, the Emperor, similarly represents the solid material plane.

Number 5 symbolizes man standing midway between 1 and 10. The pentagram or five-pointed star also represents Man, with his head in the sky and his arms and legs outstretched. This figures reversed, with the head down, denotes the evil aspects of man that cause chaos and destruction. This number represents the five fingers and the five senses. Five is the number of temptation—humanity swayed first by one impulse and then by another. It is the number of generation, sex, and reproduction, and these must be uplifted to the regenerative plane symbolized by Number 10 if man would gain his heritage of eternal life.

In the Bible we read that Joshua killed five kings and hanged them in a cave, which symbolized the subjection of his five physical senses to his Will. The senses are like kings, and will rule us if we allow them to dominate. Jesus had five wounds, suggesting the suffering that has been experienced before spirit is resurrected and becomes the master.

Number 5 can also mean man dominating the physical plane beneath him and reaching up to higher realms. In this last meaning we find a relationship to Tarot Key 5, the Hierophant. As a priestly figure he represents Man in his divine as well as human aspects.

Number 6 represents the Divine or Christ-force in nature—the force behind evolution, the urge to perfection inherent in every living thing. In Number 6 we have the higher soul principle added to the merely human of Number 5. The Egyptians considered Number 6 as the symbol of generation. Expressed by two interlaced triangles, one pointed up and the other down, this symbol has been called the Seal of Solomon. Six has also been called the number of marriage, and it is associated with labor because of the six days of the labor of Creation. It also means cooperation, reciprocal action. This meaning is perhaps more apparent in those renderings of the Tarot (other than the Rider Pack used here) that show Key 6, the Lovers, as a young man trying to choose between two women, with Cupid and his arrow poised above them. In Key 6 of our Tarot cards, its mundane meaning is also the concept of choice, and its higher meaning the cooperation between the conscious and unconscious minds.

Number 7 is the number of perfection, the most sacred of all numbers. The Egyptians considered it the symbol of life eternal. The Number 7 is composed of the triad (3) and the tetrad (4), or God and nature combined in man. The importance and the favorable aspects of Number 7 have been handed down from the days of the Chaldeans in the game of dice, the opposite sides of which always add up to 7. Both the Old and New Testaments are filled with references to 7, particularly in the Book of Revelation, which used 7 to show completion: 7 vials of the 7 last plagues, 7 trumpet calls, 7 angels, 7 kings, and the beast with 7 heads. In Tarot Key 7, the Chariot, we have completion, in the sense that the charioteer is the conqueror and the corrector of imbalance.

Number 8 is the number of evolution; its symbol is the hourglass and the balance. Since evolution can advance only by reaping that which is sown, Number 8 is a perfect symbol of balance or cause and effect. Also, in 8 we enter a higher cycle of evolution. In the majority of Tarot renderings, Key 8 is the card Justice, which would be closer to the numerological connotations. In this pack, Justice is Key 11. One questions why A. E. Waite, who had this Rider Pack drawn to his design, transposed Key 11, Strength, with Key 8. In his book *The Pictorial Key to the Tarot*, he says, "For reasons which satisfy myself, this card has been interchanged with that of Justice, which is usually numbered eight. As the variation carries nothing with it which will signify to the reader, there is no cause for explanation."

Paul Foster Case, who adapted his cards from those of Waite, also placed Strength in Key 8. He says: "In the exoteric Tarot, Key 8 is Justice and Key 11, Strength. This blind does not mislead those who know the attributions of the signs of the zodiac to the letters of the alphabet. . . . Keys 8 and 11 represent two aspects of the operation of a single power."

Remembering the cosmic lemniscate over the head of Strength, we have to conclude the woman in this card is probably maintaining a true balance of forces in controlling the lion, or lower passions, and thus properly belongs in the Key 8 position.

Number 9 is primarily the number of initiation. As the last of the digits, it is the symbol of that which brings things to an end and prepares for a new manifestation. In Key 9, the Hermit denotes the strength of maturity and the discretion of wisdom. He holds his lamp high for those below seeking initiation. The Fool is now following the lamp of Truth.

Number 10 is the number of completion. In it we meet the 0 of unmanifested force with which we started, but after it has evolved through the 9 digits. Now the first differentiation, Number 1, stands beside the 0, ready to begin a new series of manifestations on a higher cycle of evolution. Beginning with 1, we evolve until we reach the 5 of manhood. At this point we become aware of the Christ-force, 6, and begin to reach upward in evolution until we attain our initiation in 9. In Key 10, the Wheel of Fortune, the wheel represents the 0 in 10. In some cards the wheel pivots upon the upper end of an upright post—1. For the wheel to be a perfect 10, it must be balanced by Typhon and Hermes-Anubis—the pair of opposites.

Number 11 means a new beginning, but one that depends for its accomplishment upon the wisdom and efficiency acquired during the past cycle from 1 to 10. There is an 11-

year cycle to the sun. In Key 11, Justice, we are warned that we must begin the new cycle in a balanced manner, weighing out thoughts, words, and deeds on the golden scales.

Number 12 is called the number of fruition or the manifested universe. It is the sign of complete expression.

All great religions are, fundamentally, allegorical expressions of the universal Sun Myth. The stages of unfoldment of their Founders correspond to the activities of the physical Sun in nature during the cycle of 12 months. There were the 12 sons of Jacob, who founded the 12 tribes of Israel. There were the 12 princes of Ishmael, the 12 Olympian deities, the 12 apostles of Osiris, the 12 apostles of Jesus, the 12 knights of King Arthur's Round Table, and many more. They all correspond to the 12 signs of the Zodiac, with the Sun in the center.

The twelfth number is not easy to understand because its numerical composition of $10 + 2$ shows it is fruition or perfection in duality, the Number 2 indicating the physical separation into male and female, positive and negative. In Key 12, the Hanged Man, we find the lesson that man must hang upside down, with his feet where his head should be, until he accomplishes the Great Work of Regeneration within himself. He can never stand in the center and dominate the Zodiac while he hangs by one foot. Ultimately he must stand upon his feet and surmount the cross (4) with the spiritual triangle (3). He must go from $\overline{\triangledown}$ to $\triangle$, as symbolized in Key 21 by the dancing figure.

Number 13 can be dangerous, for in its negative aspect it is the number of necromancy and evocation whose power can draw to it subtle forces for evil. Number 13 expresses the perpetual movement of creation, construction, and renewal. It is the number of the vernal cross of springtime, of the zodiacal sign Aries, in which the sun commences a new cycle of life. Hence, it is the promise of immortality, the Christ in the midst of His 12 disciples. Thus, though Key 13, Death, means physical death to the unenlightened, to the initiate it means the commencement of a new life through the transformation of material desires into spiritual aspirations.

Number 14 is the number of the Mental Foundation, for it is only when the mind of man has laid a firm foundation and knows what he is to build upon that he can become a balanced producer of thought. Number 4 is the Foundation Stone of the physical, and 10 + 4 is Foundation on a higher cycle, the mental. Therefore, 14 is all that No. 4 symbolizes, with the power of 10 added. Number 14 is also 7 + 7, and just as 7 completes the first octave of creation, so 14 completes the second octave of illuminating intelligence. In Key 14, Temperance, we find man now able to pour the waters of life from one cup to another without spilling any of the precious fluid.

Number 15 combines the 10 of perfection with the 5 of humanity and also is related to the Christ-force, for 1 + 5 = 6. As soon as man realizes that he is like the Angel in Key 14, pride is likely to enter, and he is tempted to use his newfound powers for evil. The forces personified by the Devil are very real, for they are man's own creations and will disintegrate only when thought and belief are withdrawn from them. In Key 15, the Devil, man, and woman are chained through the wrong use of the Magician's magic wand; they have erected the Devil on a pedestal and are now chained to their own creation. But Number 6 is the ultimate of 15, and the Divine force must prevail. Number 15 is also the symbol of eroticism.

Number 16 indicates Spiritual victory for the 10 of completion, plus the 6 of the Divine force, which manifest Number 7 in perfection. The Number 16 is sacred to the Sun and is called the solar light. Here the Divine force is struggling with matter—tearing down, disintegrating, so that higher and more perfect forms can be built. In Key 16, the Tower, we see the Divine Sun-force at work tearing down that which has been built by pride, ignorance, and false reasoning.

Number 17 expresses the interior light that illuminates; 10 + 7 indicates another place of rest, but this time farther up the mountain. Here it is time for Man to stop and meditate, and recognize that he himself has now become a creator through the use of his imagination, for to imagine a thing

is firmly to create a model of what is desired, perfect in all
its details. In Key 17, the Star, we see this idea very clearly
depicted as the kneeling woman listens to the voice of inner
direction.

Number 18 implies the exploration of secret realms—a quest
that is not without its perils and is a warning that the path
should be attempted only by those who have come to this
second initiation. Number 8 is evolution, and leads to
$1 + 8 = 9$, initiation. Or it can be thought of as $6 + 6 + 6$
$= 18$, and then it would refer to the initiation not only of
the individual but also of the race. The evolving soul must
hold tight to his Rod of Power, and remember it is the
spiritual force that is the sustainer of all Manifestation. In
Key 18, the Moon, we see that there are many hidden things
to be learned, even by those who are already advanced on
the Path.

Number 19 is the number of ultimate attainment, both as
19 and as $1 + 9 = 10$. Man, in Key 18, was initiated into
the mysteries of the moon or the hidden side of Nature; now
he is the Sun initiate, ready to accomplish on the inner
plane that which is comparable to the work the Sun accomplishes on earth. In Key 19, the Sun, we have a complete
out-picturing of that which Key 1, the Magician, suggested—
the completion of the Great Work.

Number 20 is composed of two complete cycles of 10, each
containing the experiences of the 9 digits. But, unlike 10,
which has 1 standing beside the 0 of unmanifested forces,
in 20 we have a 2, the expression of duality. Here the 2 is
not a number denoting separation or departure, but is made
up of two 1's—God and Man united in one figure. It indicates rebirth into complete oneness with Divine power. In
Tarot Key 20, Judgment, the meaning of the card is
definitely resurrection and renewal, the figures arising from
their coffins of materiality and being reborn of the spirit.

Number 21 indicates the completion of the second cycle of
10 and the beginning of a new cycle of angelhood,
$3 \times 7 = 21$, the highest possible development of the adept
(7). Here man and woman are no longer separate personali-

ties, having been drawn into the Higher Self upon completion of their separate cycles in 20. In Tarot Key 21, the World, we see the Soul after it has completed its earthly passage and is now cocreator with the Divine force.

In the Minor Arcana, the meanings of the cards follow along with Numerology to some extent, but they are much more clearly related to the ten Sephiroth of the Tree of Life. This is more fully discussed in the section on the Tarot and the Kabalah.

The Tarot and the Kabalah

The Kabalah is a collection of ancient mystical concepts, the purpose of which was to connect a finite universe with an infinite God, to account for the existence of evil, and to point to a way of spiritual attainment. The essential meaning of the Kabalah is concentrated in the Tree of Life, which shows the Eternal One as the entire consciousness of existence, limiting itself to suit every form of Its creation.

The rabbis of antiquity prided themselves on possessing what they claimed was the "Secret Knowledge," which God gave Moses for the exclusive use of the priesthood, in contradistinction to the "Written Law" intended for the masses of the people. At first it was handed down by word of mouth from Hebrew prophet to prophet, and it was not until around A.D. 600 that sections of the Kabalah were transcribed on parchment by learned rabbis in various parts of Europe. About A.D. 900, a Hebrew philosopher and translator of the Bible composed a commentary on one section of the Kabalah, called *The Sepher Yetzirah* (The Book of Formation), and it is with this section that we are concerned. After it had been written down and other commentaries on it were available, the Kabalah came to be known to scholars in Europe, and Kabalistic schools developed in France, Germany, and Spain.

Modern scholars, influenced by the rationalizations of Maimonides, which dismissed the emotions, have looked askance at the Kabalah. The trend in the last century was toward some skepticism and disapproval. Now, as we approach the Aquarian Age, many have become disillusioned with materialistic and purely scientific philosophies and are turning again to things of the spirit. The Kabalah and its millennial wisdom were found to embody a complete philosophy that had not only withstood the centuries but was still offering illuminated answers about who we are, where we came from, and what the purpose of life is.

The whole subject, however, has been deliberately confused by those who originally put the Kabalah into writing. To throw the beginning student off the track, they used all the allusions and heavily veiled meanings of the oral Kabalah —even the "blinds" or deliberate pieces of misinformation. It was only later, during oral instruction, that these "blinds" were corrected for those who were considered true initiates. Modern minds accustomed to think in straight lines may feel initially that the Kabalah resembles a medieval crossword puzzle too difficult to solve, but there is a real challenge in tracing out the clues in the written material and finding its hidden meanings.

THE TREE OF LIFE

The kernel of the Kabalah is the Tree of Life, a diagram of symbols that enables the everyday consciousness to communicate with the subconscious and also with the superconscious. This thought is brought out in Tarot Key 6, the Lovers. The Tree should not be thought of as only a design on paper but as a three-dimensional living universe.

The Tree of Life contains ten globes called Sephiroth, which start at the top of the Tree with No. 1 and progress down to No. 10. Each Sephirah has a name as well as a number. (It will be helpful to study the accompanying diagrams as you read.)

All the aspects of the Tree of Life are called Paths, "the 32 Paths of Concealed Glory"; the Sephiroth themselves represent the Paths from 1 to 10. Actually, the connecting links between the Sephiroth are the true paths, 22 of them, numbered from 11 to 32 (shown on Diagram 5 by the double lines).

Above the Tree are three curved lines. The one at the top represents Ain—Absolute Nothing, the NIL. Next comes Ain Soph—Total Light; the lowest is Ain Soph Aur—Limitless Light. These are the three aspects of zero, 0, which precede No. 1, Kether. Kether might be called CAUSE; the next eight Sephiroth can be thought of as the MEANS by which, in Malkuth, No. 10, we have the final effect. The Kabalah

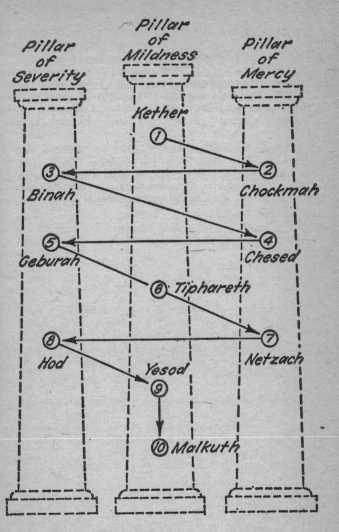

Diagram 4: THE PILLARS ON THE TREE OF LIFE

attempts to symbolize the emanation of ALL from Ain by using the analogy of Light. First, the Nothing—NIL, in which ALL IS; then coming down into expression in Kether, condensed Light. This idea is suggested in Genesis: "And the Spirit of God moved upon the face of the waters [the subconscious, the yet unformed]. And God said, Let there be light: and there was light." It has been said that the entire Bible can be more fully understood after a study of the Kabalah.

The Paths between the ten Sephiroth are channels that partake of the meanings of the two Sephiroth they connect. Tiphareth, Sephirah No. 6, is the vital center of the Tree; it will be noticed that 21 of the Paths connect with it. Here the Light of Kether shines directly down the middle Pillar and becomes the Life-light in Tiphareth. This is as high as man can reach as an evolved human being—the Christ-Buddha attainment—and this is as low on the Tree as Spirit can penetrate.

THE PILLARS

The importance of the idea of balance cannot be overemphasized in dealing with the Tree of Life and the message it has for us. Balance is indicated by the three Pillars that control the Sephiroth. The right-hand Pillar is called Mercy; the one on the left, Severity; and, to balance these two aspects of life, there is the middle Pillar, Mildness. (Diagram 4.)

The Pillar of Mercy is considered positive or masculine. For example, Chesed, Mercy, attains its proper function when it is ordering and preserving all things harmoniously; used wrongly, mercy becomes sentimentality and preserves those things that might better be destroyed.

The Pillar of Severity is negative or feminine. At the head of the Pillar is Binah, the Great Mother, who can be considered to be performing the proper function when providing stability and endurance, but not when Binah's resistance is so great that it turns into active aggression and begets obstruction. The middle Pillar symbolizes the consciousness of Man, which must learn to balance the positive and negative aspects of life.

THE FOUR WORLDS

The ten Sephiroth operate from Nil to material manifestation through what the Kabalists called the Four Worlds or Stages. These are Atziluth, the world of archetypes where all begins to be something; Briah, where creation takes place; Yetzirah, where formation occurs; and Assiah, the material world. Each Sephirah then is, in a sense, divided into four sections in which each of the Four Worlds operates.

Thus we have the ten Sephiroth, the 22 Paths, the three Pillars, and the Four Worlds, and these relate to the Tarot cards in this way: The ten Sephiroth relate to the numbered cards 1 to 10 of the Minor Arcana; the Four Worlds to the four suits; the 22 Paths to the 22 cards of the Major Arcana.

THE TEN SEPHIROTH

No. 1—*Kether, the Crown*

This first Sephirah symbolizes the hitherto unmanifest at the point where it can become knowable to us. In Kether, there is still no form, only pure Being or Life in a state of inertia; but latent within it there are both male and female potentialities. As Pure Being it stands behind manifestation and projects it. Here the pairs of opposites have not yet declared themselves, as they do in Chokmah and Binah; in Tiphareth they have finally arrived at perfect equilibrium.

No. 2—*Chokmah, Wisdom, the Crown of Creation*

Here we find the virile force that gives impulse to manifestation. The first three Sephiroth are called by Kabalists the Three Supernals, and it is here that sex has its roots, for it is cosmic and spiritual. It is between Chokmah, primordial maleness, and Binah, the primordial femaleness, that the web of life is woven. Chokmah is the great stimulator of the universe, the positive male force.

No. 3—*Binah, Understanding, the Throne*

Binah is negative, and thus able to receive the positive flow from Chokmah. She is the great Mother of the Universe, but she is also at the top of the Pillar of Severity, for the embodied spirit sees death on the horizon as soon as it is born. The idea of experiencing sorrow and death is implicit in the descent of life into form. The seed planted in the earth dies that it may multiply, so Binah is death for the Chokmah force and truly belongs on the Pillar of Severity.

The next six Sephiroth are what the Kabalists call the Lesser Countenance of the Cosmos on a lower plane. Here we find the forces of growth and abundance.

No. 4—Chesed, Mercy, Majesty

We can call Chokmah the "all-begetter" in the abstract, and Chesed the same power in a more concrete form as the loving father, the protector, and preserver. All the creative work in the world is done by people whose minds work in terms of Chesed the King, seated on his throne and holding both scepter and orb. He is the benevolent ruler who also guides his people. This idea is symbolized in Tarot Key 4, the Emperor. He has become master of the world of abstract ideas and can select images to fit his purpose and bring them down into the concrete plane of Malkuth.

No. 5—Geburah, Strength, Severity

Just as Chesed, the father of his people in times of peace, may win our love, it is Geburah, the King in his chariot going forth to war, who commands our respect. Here is the fear of the Lord (Law), which is the beginning of wisdom. Geburah represents the breaking-down force that is necessary for the equilibrium of the Tree of Life. Like Vishnu and Shiva, the preservers and terminators of life, Geburah and Chesed are indispensable to each other. One builds and the other breaks down in an endless cyclic relationship, in order to maintain balance. Here we find the warlike qualities of Mars, which is Saturn on a lower arc.

What we call evil is simply misplaced force—misplaced in both time and space—just as fire can bring either welcome warmth or destruction. In most instances, we have been taught that which is constructive and builds up is good; that which is destructive and breaks down is evil. But a piece of furniture cannot be built unless a tree is felled; a garden cannot grow unless the weeds are removed. Love can be either a blessing or a curse. Here we have the all-important concept of balance and its applicability in every phase of life.

The Tarot suit of Swords is related to Geburah, as both represent the destructive aspect of life.

No. 6—*Tiphareth, Beauty, Harmony, a Sacrificed God*

Tiphareth, on the central Pillar of equilibrium, has the balance of Kether on a lower plane and that of Yesod on the higher one. The three Sephiroth below Tiphareth represent the personality or lower self; the four above Tiphareth, the individuality or higher Self; and above them all is Kether, the Divine Spark that sets Life in motion. Tiphareth is also the point of change from the planes of force above it to those of form below. This sixth Sephirah is called the child of Kether and the King of Malkuth, and in his own sphere he is sacrificed. Sacrifice here means the transmutation of force from one form to another. When we make a sacrifice of any sort, we take one form of expression and channel it into another. We gladly sacrifice time, money, and pleasure that these may be transmuted into higher forms of accomplishment.

In Tiphareth, God is made manifest in form, and dwells among us; Tiphareth, the Son, "shows us" Kether, the Father, and this idea is perfectly equilibrated, for the mediator or redeemer is ever striving to bring balance to his kingdom by reuniting the higher Sephiroth with the lower. Incarnated gods are sacrificed, in the sense that they die for the people in order that the tremendous emotional force set free by this act may bring about an equilibrium of forces.

It is this Sephirah on the Tree of Life that the Christian religion takes as its focusing point. The pantheistic faiths, such as those of the Greeks and the Egyptians, center in Yesod; and the metaphysical faiths, such as those of the Buddhists, Confucians, and—in this age—the New Thought Movement, aim at Kether. The Bible is essentially a Kabalistic book, as indicated in the fact that allusions to the Son refer to Tiphareth; the Father, to Kether, and the Holy Ghost, to Yesod.

Helios, Osiris, and all the sun gods also have their abode at Tiphareth; it is through the sun that life comes to earth, and it is by means of the God-consciousness or Tiphareth that we contact the sources of vitality and are able to draw upon them. The understanding of outward (exoteric) religion goes no farther up the Tree than Tiphareth, and has no grasp of the mysteries of creation.

No. 7—*Netzach, Victory, Force, Venus-Aphrodite*

The victory here is the victory of achievement. Netzach represents force on the lower plane, Chokmah on the higher. This Sephirah contains two ideas—one, power or force, as exemplified by Mars; two, the beauty of Venus. Their connection is exemplified in the old myth of the love between Mars and Venus. Netzach is also the sphere of the artist, who expresses the emotions and instincts in sound and color. Here, in No. 7 and No. 8, we again have a pair of opposites—Netzach, the artist in us; Hod, the scientist. The force of Netzach needs the form of Hod in order to express, and they both pour their energy into Yesod.

No. 8—*Hod, Splendor, Form, Intelligence*

Hod is on the left Pillar, which is passive and female in that it brings the force from the right Pillar into form. The three upper Sephiroth form a triangle pointing upward; the next three, a downward triangle, which is that of the individuality. The third triangle, also pointing downward, is that of manifestation and personality. Hod is the sphere of Mercury-Hermes, the god of science and books, who works in the mental realm in a scientific manner; Hod is the scientist in us as Netzach is the artist.

No. 9—*Yesod, Storehouse of Images, the Foundation*

Yesod is the receptacle of the emanations of all the other Sephiroth and the transmitter of these to the physical plane. It is the function of Yesod to purify these emanations and correct them when necessary before they are passed down into the earth plane of Malkuth. In Yesod there is the energy of integration, which coordinates the physical molecules and cells into definite organisms. Living creatures, plants, and even minerals are its products, though the images are still in the prephysical state.

Yesod is also the sphere of Maya—illusion, magic, and psychism as distinguished from the religious mysticism of Tiphareth. This is the Sephirah we first encounter when we try to rise above the purely physical—Malkuth. It is, in a sense, the great subconscious filled from time immemorial with images that we may encounter in our first attempts at meditation.

No. 10—*Malkuth, the Kingdom, Stability*

This Sephirah, at the base of the pillar of equilibrium, represents the entire physical world, which receives the emanations from all other Sephiroth after they have been corrected and purified in Yesod. Malkuth is divided into the four substances necessary for energy to be encased: Air, Earth, Fire, and Water. Therefore, Yesod, the form-giver, depends for manifestation on the substance provided by Malkuth.

According to occult teaching, man descends involuntarily from Kether, picking up functional aspects of his personality in each Sephirah as he descends, until he arrives at Malkuth, the kingdom of *this* world, the end result of the Divine pattern. Life on the earth plane is to be lived and enjoyed and learned from—a definite stage in soul development that each must traverse and learn to control before he attempts to ascend the ladder of Sephiroth, to rest again in Kether.

THE MINOR ARCANA AND THE TREE OF LIFE

It seems clear that the Minor Arcana have distinct correspondences not only to the Sephiroth but also to the Four Worlds of the Kabalists. As previously noted, when the number four is used it almost invariably refers to the four letters of the name of Jehovah, IHVH, and to the four corners of the earth, as well as the four elements: Fire, Water, Air, and Earth.

Each of the ten Sephiroth is theoretically divided into four segments to denote that each of the Four Worlds works in each of the Sephiroth.

ATZILUTH	God works directly through archetypes	Fire	Wands
BRIAH	Creation takes place through archangels	Air	Swords
YETZIRAH	Formation occurs through angels	Water	Cups

ASSIAH   Material world works   Earth   Pentacles
              through elements and
              signs of the Zodiac

In the four Tarot suits the cards are numbered from one to ten, corresponding to the similarly numbered Sephiroth. The four aces are assigned to Kether, the first Sephirah; the four Twos to Chokmah; the four Threes to Binah; and so on down to the four Tens, assigned to Malkuth—the Wands still keeping their association with fire, Cups with water, Swords with air, and Pentacles with earth. Each suit represents the action of one of the Four Worlds in relation to its numbered Sephirah.

For example, the Three of Cups and the third Sephirah, Binah, reinforce each other, for both Cups and Binah represent fertility. The Three of Swords, a heart pierced by swords, represents the destructive force latent in Binah, as further exemplified by the Hindu goddess of destruction, Shiva. The whole suit of Swords has to do with strife and misfortune, and when the Five of Swords falls on Geburah, the breaking-down force, we have a card of double trouble. Cups are good cards on the whole, but the Five of this suit on Geburah shows loss and frustration.

Malkuth is on the plane of dense matter, so here the tens of the four suits must relate to it. The Kabalists say that what is outwardly solar is inwardly corrosive, and what is outwardly corrosive is inwardly solar. Cups and Pentacles are outwardly solar and are thus alike in showing good and happy qualities in the tens—which relate to Malkuth. But this is a warning that they can be inwardly corrosive, and the good they portray may not be lasting. Wands and swords are inwardly solar and outwardly corrosive, so we find the tens in both these suits to be the extreme of sorrow and misfortune, but these conditions do not last, and those who have been tried by sorrow will eventually find their happiness.

THE COURT CARDS

The four Court cards of each Tarot suit have also been assigned to the Four Worlds, but in a different arrangement. The Sephiroth on the Central Pillar are the most important, and as there are four of them, they are correlated with the Four Worlds and with the four Court cards. Kabalists feel that the Knight's being on horseback makes him of more importance than the King, who in this instance is relegated to the usual place of the Knight—as the son of the Queen and the Knight. It therefore goes: Atziluth works in Kether as the Knight, Briah in Tiphareth as the Queen, Yetzirah in Yesod as the King, and Assiah in Malkuth as the Page.

The varying designs of the Court cards, being highly conventionalized, make this correlation of doubtful value. Certainly for divination or even a study of the Tarot, the above does not seem helpful. However, studying the Tarot cards from 1 to 10 along with the meanings of the Sephiroth and the Four Worlds gives an understanding of why some cards have been designated as "good cards" and others as "bad cards." If the meanings of the Sephiroth are kept in mind, any pack of modern playing cards can be used for divination.

THE TREE OF LIFE AND THE MAJOR ARCANA

The Major Arcana are involved not so much with the Sephiroth as with the 22 Paths between them, which correspond to the 22 letters of the Hebrew alphabet. Each of the Keys of the Major Arcana is assigned to a Hebrew letter and to a Path. The meanings of the cards partake of the influences of both the connecting Sephiroth.

The Table of Paths gives the number of the Path, the two Sephiroth it connects, its assigned Hebrew letter as well as the Tarot Key, and its astrological sign. This particular assignment of Tarot Keys to the Paths was chosen because it is the one most commonly accepted. It is the arrangement decided on by members of the Order of the Golden Dawn and by those who have followed their interpretations.

A reminder may be in order here that the "Paths proper" begin with No. 11 and go on to 32, since the ten Sephiroth are thought of as the first ten Paths. Thus the Fool, 0, is allocated to the Hebrew letter Aleph (A) and the 11th Path.

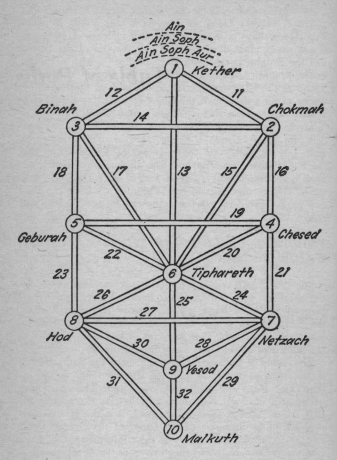

Diagram 5: THE TREE OF LIFE (WITH PATHS)

Table of Paths

PATHS	SEPHIROTH	HEBREW LETTER	TAROT KEY	ASTRO-LOGICAL SYMBOL
11	Kether—Chokmah	Aleph	The Fool	Air
12	Kether—Binah	Beth	The Magician	Mercury
14	Binah—Chokmah	Daleth	The Empress	Venus
16	Chesed—Chokmah	Vav	The Hierophant	Taurus
18	Geburah—Binah	Cheth	The Chariot	Cancer
15	Tiphareth—Chokmah	Heh	The Star	Aries
17	Tiphareth—Binah	Zain	The Lovers	Gemini
13	Tiphareth—Kether	Gimel	The High Priestess	Moon
23	Hod—Geburah	Mem	The Hanged Man	Water
21	Netzach—Chesed	Kaph	Wheel of Fortune	Jupiter
19	Geburah—Chesed	Teth	Strength	Leo
22	Tiphareth—Geburah	Lamed	Justice	Libra
20	Tiphareth—Chesed	Yod	The Hermit	Virgo
24	Netzach—Tiphareth	Nun	Death	Scorpio

PATHS	SEPHIROTH	HEBREW LETTER	TAROT KEY	ASTRO-LOGICAL SYMBOL
26	Hod—Tiphareth	Ayin	The Devil	Capricorn
25	Yesod—Tiphareth	Samech	Temperance	Sagittarius
27	Hod—Netzach	Peh	The Tower	Mars
30	Yesod—Hod	Resh	The Sun	The Sun
28	Yesod—Netzach	Tzaddi	The Emperor	Aquarius
31	Malkuth—Hod	Shin	Judgment	Fire
29	Malkuth—Netzach	Qoph	The Moon	Pisces
32	Malkuth—Yesod	Tau	The Universe	Saturn

The important meaning of both the Tree of Life and the Tarot is the equilibration of the positive and negative aspects of life. Small differences of opinion as to the placement of the Keys on the Path, or correlating them to the Hebrew alphabet are incidental and cannot rob either of their true importance.

SOME TAROT KEYS TO PATHS

The 11th Path, Chokmah—Kether, Hebrew letter "Aleph"

The Fool is the Tarot Key assigned to this Path, for he is a great archetype that is embedded in the race subconscious and appears often in myth and fairy tale. He is Sir Dagonet, the jester of King Arthur, and also appears as the medieval fool or court jester; in modern times he is exemplified by a Charlie Chaplin. The Fool is wise as well as foolish—perhaps using his foolishness as a means of instruction in wisdom while appearing to be an innocent idiot in the ordinary world. Some may even consider Jesus a fool to have let Himself be crucified when He could have saved Himself.

Kether contains the seed of all life, and its descent into

Chokmah is the first move of power, symbolized by the lightning flash. This is the Path of the illumined soul who sees God face to face; the ascent from Chokmah to Kether is the final approach to union with God.

The 25th Path, Yesod—Tipareth, Hebrew letter "Samech"

Tarot Key 14, Temperance, shows an angel pouring the waters of life from a silver cup (moon—Yesod) into a golden one (sun—Tiphareth), the higher meaning of this card being the tempering of the soul to make it a fit vessel for higher illumination.

The irises growing beside the pool represent the goddess of the rainbow, Iris, and the rainbow the sign of God's covenant with man that "the waters shall no more become a flood to destroy all flesh" (Genesis 9:15). In the context of the 25th Path, it would seem to be a promise that man can become a fully illuminated being.

In like manner, the student can work out for himself the positions on the Tree of Life of the other Keys of the Major Arcana, and in this way additional light will be thrown onto the meanings of the cards.

The Tarot and Astrology

The Zodiac is probably the oldest recorded philosophic concept, dating back (it is said) at least 48,000 years. The Great Pyramid at Ghizah was constructed in line with astrological calculations so that the main passage leading down to the King's chamber was angled to permit the rays from the polar star of that age to shine down the passage and rest upon the sarcophagus in the center of the chamber.

The Greeks, and later the Romans, followed the astrological knowledge of the ancient Persians, Chaldeans, and Assyrians. After the fall of Rome in A.D. 475, the eastern empire, with its capital in Byzantium, still carried on the study of Astrology and used it for divination. As the Arabs grew in power, they developed many able astrologers; Arabic textbooks on the subject were studied as late as the seventeenth century.

The literature of the Middle Ages is full of references to Astrology. Indeed, the basic structure of Dante's *Divine Comedy* is astrological. Dante, accompanied by Virgil, starts on his wanderings when the Sun is in Aries (which rules new beginnings) ; he comes to Purgatory when the Sun is in Scorpio, the sign of regeneration. He comes to the top of Purgatory when the Sun is in Taurus, the sign of Earthly Paradise. In the Paradiso he journeys through the seven planets, learning the lessons and feeling the deep joys of each.

Astrologers through the centuries have tried to predict the arrival of new world teachers and new epochs of civilization through adding to and subtracting from Biblical dates. The Aquarian Age is said to have started in A.D. 1882, but this date cannot be fixed as there is still considerable controversy as to the date of the beginning of the Piscean Age. So

much was predicted about the Second Coming that the
Crusades were preached in every country of Europe as a
Christian duty, to clear the Holy Land of infidels before
Christ's arrival. Perhaps the whole episode of the Crusades
can be laid at the feet of astrologers.

In England, Geoffrey Chaucer was considered a very fine
astrologer; his poem *Canterbury Tales* abounds in astrological symbolism. Before she was queen, Elizabeth I had
her horoscope calculated by Lord Burghley and he saw in
the stars that she would come to the throne in spite of all
her enemies. A group of distinguished scholars used to meet
in a tavern in Gunpowder Alley in London to discuss not
only Astrology but the Kabalah. One of the group was
William Lilly, who translated astrological books from the
Latin to make them more available. His textbook *Introduc-
tion to Astrology* is still widely read. Over ten years before
the Great Fire of London (1666) and the Great Plague
(1663), Lilly predicted their exact date.

In the eighteenth century a number of notable authors are
said to have been interested in Astrology—Byron, Shelley,
Scott, and Goethe. In both the nineteenth and twentieth
centuries the astrologers worked on assigning characteristics
and substances to the new planets, Uranus, Neptune, and
Pluto, and research of this kind still goes on. Some
astrologers took names other than their own, such as
Raphael, Zuriel, Neptune, and Sepharial.

The works of Alan Leo (1860–1917), a profound astrologer
as well as a mathematician, are still standard textbooks.
Evangeline Adams (1865–1932) made horoscopes for the
great of both continents. She was also a palmist, and while
doing a chart for a client she always wanted to look at his
hands. Llewellyn George and Grant Lewi are two others
well known for their astrological books in the early nineteen hundreds.

We have said that Astrology had its beginning in pre-
history, and that little is known of the precise time when the
Tarot originated. In any case, there is a recurrent correlation between the meanings of the cards and those of the
zodiacal symbols; at times the Tarot and Astrology appear to
be different branches of the same discipline. For the last
two hundred years, the Tarot has been written about and
discussed by masters of the occult as they tried to rediscover

the meanings lost during those centuries when the cards had largely been used by Gypsies in fortunetelling. Apparently the Tarot was initiated secretly during the Dark Ages, in the face of a repression of which Astrology, too, was a victim.

But at best there were only scattered groups of men in widely separated places concentrating on such occult pursuits as the Tarot, alchemy, Astrology, and the Kabalah. The Tarot cards were like pages of an unbound book compiled to show man's place in the universe, how the laws of God work, and the steps a man must take to become an initiate in the Mystery Schools. They chose from the lore of the Kabalah, from Astrology and Numerology, from the mythology of the Egyptians, the Indians, the Hebrews, and the Greeks, selecting only those symbols that seemed to be of universal meaning. These they concealed in picture cards that were used in games of chance and in fortunetelling, where they remained hidden until the savants of the eighteenth century got to work on them and redeciphered their original meanings.

The section on "The Tarot and the Kabalah" shows the Tree of Life, its ten Sephiroth and their meanings and relationships. The four suits of the Tarot cards and their numbers from ace to ten were shown in their relation to the Sephiroth. The 22 paths that run between the Sephiroth, the 22 letters of the Hebrew alphabet, and the 22 cards of the Major Arcana were also shown to have related meanings.

Efforts have been made by occultists to correlate the Major Arcana with astrological symbols. There are twelve signs of the Zodiac and seven planets; since this adds up to only nineteen, the three elements Air, Fire, and Water, have been included. (The element Earth has been omitted, since it goes with Malkuth.)

There is some disagreement among the writers on the Tarot who have attempted to correlate the cards with astrological symbols. One of the reasons for the disagreement is the placement of Key 0, the Fool. Some placed the Fool before Key 1, the Magician (as we have done); some put the Fool just before Key 21, the Universe, and others just after it. Some have switched the positions of Key 8, Strength, and Key 11, Justice; and others have also reversed the places of Key 4, the Emperor, and Key 17, the Star. Justice, Key

11, has been assigned at various times to Capricorn, to Libra, and to Aquarius. Each writer makes a relatively plausible case for his own designations, though he sometimes goes far afield to make his point.

The followers of the Order of the Golden Dawn have assigned the Major Arcana to the Paths between the Sephiroth, which works out well enough with the Kabalistic meanings; we do not, however, go along with the astrological symbols they have allocated to the Paths and the Tarot. These astrological designations are shown in the Table of Paths. After some study, we have devised a different system, which we call the Three-Dimensional, that should satisfy both astrologers and Tarotists—and also, we hope, the Kabalists, for we still use the Tree of Life to hang our symbols on.

THE THREE-DIMENSIONAL TREE

The Tree of Life does not necessarily have to be thought of as a flat, two-dimensional design, and so for our purpose we think of it as a globe turning on an axis. The axis begins above the globe at Kether and runs through it, touching Tiphareth and emerging at Malkuth. At the center of this imaginary globe, which should be thought of as suspended in the air, we have the Sun, and, around it in their orbits, the seven planets. Each planet has been assigned to a Sephirah and also to a Tarot Key. (Follow this closely on Diagram 6.)

(1) KETHER, the Fool, No. 0 (no planet)
(2) CHOKMAH, the Universe, No. XXI (all zodiacal signs)
(3) BINAH, Death, No. XIII, Saturn
(4) CHESED, the Emperor, No. IV, Jupiter
(5) GEBURAH, the Tower, No. XVI, Mars
(6) TIPHARETH, the Hanged Man, No. XII, the Sun
(7) NETZACH, the Empress, No. III, Venus
(8) HOD, the Magician, No. I, Mercury
(9) YESOD, the High Priestess, No. II, Moon
(10) MALKUTH, Wheel of Fortune, No. X, the Four Elements

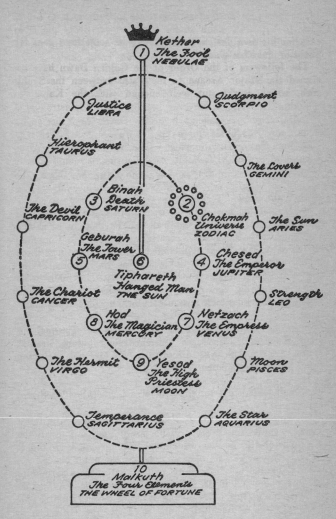

Diagram 6: THE THREE-DIMENSIONAL TREE

On the Outer Circle

Around this globe, in a moving band or circle, are the 12 signs of the Zodiac and their matching Tarot cards:

Judgment, No. XX, Scorpio
The Lovers, No. VI, Gemini
The Sun, No. XIX, Aries
Strength, No. VIII, Leo
The Moon, No. XVIII, Pisces
The Star, No. XVII, Aquarius
Temperance, No. XIV, Sagittarius

The Hermit, No. IX, Virgo
The Chariot, No. VII, Cancer
The Devil, No. XV, Capricorn
The Hierophant, No. V, Taurus
Justice, No. XI, Libra

Kether, the Crown . . . the Fool

Kether, at the top of the axis, is pure being, all-potential but nonactive. The first Sephirah can be thought of as the preexplosive power behind created existence, and Chokmah as the explosion that is regulated by Binah. These first three Sephiroth are called the Supernals, as they represent the initial stages of life as consciousness only. The Fool, in its esoteric meaning, goes along with Kether, as they both represent the unknown absolute before it comes into manifestation.

Some have linked the Fool with the planet Uranus, but since the Tarot came into existence long before Uranus, Pluto, or Neptune was discovered, we are not including them in our arrangement.

Chokmah, Wisdom . . . the Universe . . . (all 12 zodiacal signs)

Chokmah is the spirit of *all* wisdom. It is not a *form* but a *force* straight from Kether. This power goes out to all the 12 signs of the Zodiac, which we have grouped around it for clarity—as well as placing them on the outer circle.

In Chokmah we have both primal paternity and infinite wisdom expanded in an infinite universe. Thus the Temple of Wisdom is supported by twelve, not seven, pillars, and these are the zodiacal divisions. Key 21, the Universe, is assigned to Chokmah, for we have four living figures representing the four fixed signs of the Zodiac: the Eagle for Scorpio—air; the man or angel for Aquarius—water; the

lion for Leo—fire; the bull for Taurus—earth. These figures
are repeated in the Wheel of Life assigned to Malkuth, where
they are found in their mundane aspect. The wreath in the
card represents the universe, and the dancer the free Life-
force on its eternal dance.

Binah, Understanding . . . Death . . . Saturn

Here is the Supernal Mother representing the female
potency of the universe, even as Chokmah represents the
male. An old attribution of the Zodiac links Space with
Chokmah and Time with Binah. Space certainly is a dimen-
sion of the universe—the male aspect scattering his seed;
Binah, the mother aspect, needs time to bring forth that
which Chokmah has planted within her. Binah is also at the
head of the Pillar of Severity, for she has another aspect—
death (since that which is brought into form must, in the
course of time, come to the point of death and dissolution).

The planet assigned to Binah is Saturn, which here symbolizes the law of limitation that gives shape to life by
crystallization. Saturn also translates force into form, as
does Binah. Saturn has nine moons—another reason to asso-
ciate it with the Mother Principle.

Tarot Key 13, Death, fits in very well with the symbolism
of Saturn, including that of death along with the concept
of rebirth and renewal. Binah, in a sense, is the opposer of
the force from Chokmah, and by confining it to form, it is
thought by some to be the enemy of Kether, the originator
of the force. So we have Saturn-Satan and again Time-
Death-Devil. However, the Kabalah teaches that all the
Sephiroth are holy and that each performs a necessary
function, so Binah is never thought of as evil but as merely
carrying out the duties assigned to her in the overall picture
of a balanced universe.

Chesed, Love, Mercy, Majesty . . . the Emperor . . . Jupiter

Chesed is the benevolent king on his throne who brings
prosperity and happiness, his philanthropy always proceed-
ing from compassion and generosity. Jupiter is his planet,
for Jupiter has many of the same characteristics, including
expansion, justice, law, governing for the good of the governed. Tarot Key 4, the Emperor, is just such a benevolent
king.

Geburah, Severity, Strength . . . the Tower . . . Mars

When kindness and benevolence go too far they become maudlin and sentimental; then the severity of Geburah steps in to bring things to a balance. This type of justice may seem drastic and painful but it is necessary. The planet Mars, assigned to Geburah, is one that denotes both constructive and destructive energy, not only wars but the quelling of riots. The occultist does not take any extreme of society too seriously, knowing it will run its course. An extreme in either direction is at first a valuable and necessary corrective, but if it runs too far in one direction, it will swing back again like a pendulum. The very fact of an extreme having been arrived at indicates the end of the swing and its reversal.

For Geburah, we have Key 16, the Tower, where the bolt of spiritual lightning knocks the false crown off the man-made tower. The falling man and woman were in need of correction, and Geburah-Mars supplied it.

Tiphareth, Beauty, Harmony . . . the Hanged Man . . . the Sun

In the usual flat diagram of the Tree of Life, Tiphareth is halfway down the central Pillar. Here, with our three-dimensional globe, taking Tiphareth as the Sun, he is in the very center, and the planets with their Sephiroth move around him. On Diagram 5 each Sephirah except Malkuth has a Path leading to him. Tiphareth is to the Tree of Life as the Sun is to the solar system. Everything emanates from Kether, but it is Tiphareth that holds these emanations in their proper relationship to each other. Tiphareth rules as a king surrounded by his kingdom—a focusing point for the three Sephiroth below (representing the lower self or personality) and for the four above (representing the individuality or higher self), with Kether above all as the Divine Spark. The Paths on the Tree are routes for the energies arising in the Sun to pass to the other Sephiroth and for Tiphareth to receive the Supernal energy from Kether. Then the Sephiroth, in turn, exchange energies among themselves via the Paths.

To the Kabalist, evil is a condition of unbalance but not a force to be fought against as if it were directed by a powerful devil. Good is the perfect, harmonious state that is established between two polarizing principles whose forces are balanced against each other. Tiphareth on the central Pillar thus holds the balance and harmonizes the Sephiroth circling about him.

Tiphareth is called the Sphere of the Sun, and the astrological Sun is assigned here for obvious reasons. The Sun represents man's life and spirit given to him by the All-Spirit. It represents the real Self rather than Man. Here we have Tarot Key 12, the Hanged Man, one who has completely reversed his way of life from that of the ordinary man, for, in effect, he has said, "Not my will but Thine be done." At the twelfth step we find him with the triangle of Spirit below the cross of materialism. He has transmuted his lower passions into the pure gold of the Sun and ultimately will stand with the cross below the triangle. He is Osiris, the Sun god, and Yehoshua with his twelve followers. The number 12 pertains to the Great Work, which is the conquest of the personality by the individuality; the gold of spiritual realization, which is the Sun-force. By hanging from the cross of living wood, the Hanged Man symbolizes his dependence on the Spirit (Kether) above him.

Netzach, Victory, Achievement . . . the Empress . . . Venus

Netzach represents the instincts that the mind of man has here begun to transform into the emotions. Netzach is feeling, and is balanced by Hod, thinking. In Netzach all the arts that express joy are included. The planet Venus is assigned here, for Venus stands for love, beauty, desire, attraction, and the arts, including music. Venus not only brings sexual love but also the love among family members, friends, and groups. Here, our senses, emotions, and feelings are developed through the Venusian influence of Netzach. Venus has lessons to teach the heart rather than the head. Tarot Key 3, the Empress, belongs here, for both are Mother-goddesses. The Empress is the consort of the Emperor, who is just above her on the Pillar of Mercy, and she abundantly gives the fruits of her love.

Hod, Glory, Renown . . . the Magician . . . Mercury

As Netzach typifies the subconscious mind, the emotions, so Hod typifies the conscious mind, the mentality. This is the sphere of science and learning and its planet is Mercury,

who, like Hod, symbolizes adaptability—one of the first
things each must learn is to survive. The tree that bends out-
lasts the storm.

Mercury represents both the planet and the god. The
Egyptian god Hermes corresponds to the Greek god Mercury,
and Hermes is said to have written 42 books on science—
including astronomy, astrology, arithmetic, geometry, medi-
cine, music, and magic. He was also the great magician; his
caduceus survives to this day as a symbol of the healing
arts. Mercury is said to be sexless, that is, neither masculine nor feminine, whereas Hod is a hermaphrodite, one who
partakes of both sexes. The dancing figure in Tarot Key 21,
the Universe, is also thought to be a hermaphrodite (this
state was supposed to betoken a higher nature than that of
being heterosexual).

Tarot Key 1, the Magician, although it belongs to Hod
and Mercury, is a male figure representing the intellect in
the creative aspect of taking the power from above and
using it to create both the sensual, esthetic power of Venus
and the intellectual, communicating concerns of Mercury.

Yesod, the Foundation . . . the High Priestess . . . Moon

Yesod holds the framework in which the particles of
dense matter are enmeshed. It also purifies and corrects the
emanations from the other Sephiroth before passing them
down to Malkuth. It is said to hold the image of everything
that exists in the physical world, and thus it is the etheric
or psychic Sephirah in that it also holds all that man has
ever imagined.

In this aspect it is the oldest of all the vast body of beliefs
about the Moon—the reflector of the light of the Sun. Moon
myths are said to have been the foundation for modern
science. Without these myths to stir the imagination, man
might not have risen from his animal beginnings. Just as the
physical moon will be used as man's jumping-off place when
he travels to other planets, so Yesod is our jumping-off
place as we move up from Malkuth in our journey to the
starry Sephiroth.

The Moon is the planet connected with the emotions, the
subconscious, and the instinctive. It draws out of the planets
their special qualities in the same way that Yesod draws

qualities from the Sephiroth above it to fashion the personality that will appear in Malkuth. Yesod is essentially the
sphere of the Moon and, as such, comes under the guidance
of Diana, the Moon goddess. Tarot Key 2, the High Priestess,
is also a Moon goddess, and thus belongs here with Yesod.
She is also the guardian of the scroll of knowledge and
memory, which lie in the subconscious. The solar cross on
her breast shows the balancing function of Yesod in taking
what it needs from the other Sephiroth.

Malkuth, the Kingdom . . . Wheel of Fortune . . . the Four Elements

Malkuth, the final resting place, receives the influences
and emanations from all the other Sephiroth as they are
refined and adjusted in Yesod. Malkuth is the place where
force is finally locked into form. That which had its incep-
tion in Binah, the Superior Mother, has its culmination in
Malkuth, the Inferior Mother. They are not two different
types of force, but one, functioning on different levels. Think
of Malkuth as divided into four quarters, each assigned to
one of the four elements; these elements here gathered
together are the outward manifestations of all the rest.

Tarot Key 10, the Wheel of Fortune, is assigned to
Malkuth, and it is interesting to note that both their numbers are 10—a number of great significance to the Kabalist.
In the four corners of the card are the living creatures corresponding to the fixed signs of the Zodiac, the four letters
of Jehovah and the four elements:

Lion	Leo	I	Fire
Eagle	Scorpio	H	Water
Man	Aquarius	V	Air
Bull	Taurus	H	Earth

The ideas of involution and evolution are expressed in
Typhon's descent as the symbol of cosmic radiant energy
into the material world of Malkuth, while Hermes-Anubis,
the jackal-headed Egyptian god, rises on the right side of
the wheel, representing man's attempt, in consciousness, to
climb the Tree of Life to reach Chokmah. Beyond that is
Kether, where no man may go and still retain his hold on

Malkuth. Kether here appears in the guise of the Sphinx, remaining stationary while, below, ideas and force take form and then return to nothingness in an endless cycle.

THE OUTER CIRCLE

On the outer circle we have the 12 signs of the Zodiac and their corresponding Tarot cards from the Major Arcana:

Aries, the Ram . . . the Sun, No. XIX

The symbol of Aries is the horns of a ram. In Egyptian mythology Amon was united with the Sun God, and in his primitive function as a god of life and reproduction, he was represented as a ram-headed deity. Aries, the first fire sign, stands for the original cause or thunderbolt that emerged from the primordial waters. The Sun is in its exaltation in Aries, giving energy, life, and action—hence Key 19, the Sun, is assigned to Aries in our system.

Taurus, the Bull . . . the Hierophant, No. V

Taurus is an earth sign and represents stability and mature conviction—those who are retentive of what they possess, be it worldly goods or ideas. The Hierophant, Key 5, belongs to Taurus, for though he is a priest, he surrounds himself with worldly possessions; he is thought of as stable and mature in his conduct, preferring the outer forms and ritual to the invisible things of the spirit.

Gemini, the Twins . . . the Lovers, No. VI

Gemini is an air sign and also one of mentality; its keynote is equilibrium. Though the Twins suggest duality, they remain together. In Key 6, the Lovers, Raphael is the angel of the air, here representing the superconscious, showering his beneficence upon the two sides of man's nature—the conscious and the subconscious, the positive and negative aspects of personality. Raphael, by sending down his light, balances this duality.

Cancer, the Crab . . . Temperance No. XIV

The symbol of Cancer is made up of two small suns, each connected with a crescent moon, which looks like a cup or bowl. The lower cup holds water, for Cancer is a water sign; the upper cup is inverted, as if pouring water into the lower one, much like the cups held by the angel in Temperance, who pours the Water of Life from one cup to another while standing with one foot in the water and the other on land. The crab is hard on the outside and soft inside, and this is often a trait of Cancer people, who are very sensitive and emotional. Cancer is ruled by the Moon, and its people are thus often psychic.

Leo, the Lion . . . Strength, No. VIII

Leo is a fire sign and one with the power of the Sun. It

has radiance, authority, and centripetal powers. Leo draws
things to it as does the woman in Key 8, Strength, who
through her spiritual radiance controls the lion. Over her
head is the same cosmic lemniscate that is over the head of
the Magician, indicating that she has the same powers over
natural forces as symbolized here by the lion.

Virgo, the Virgin . . . the Hermit, No. IX
   In Virgo, an earth sign, there is a tendency to weigh and
consider. This is the sign of those who seek an ideal and
are not content until it is found. The Hermit who is seeking
Truth on the mountaintop is a Virgo character. Perhaps he is
not only seeking Truth for himself but also helping those
below find it, as he holds his lantern aloft.

Libra, the Scales . . . Justice, No. XI
   Libra is an air sign, and therefore mental in outlook. It
means balance, poise, and peace. What Tarot Key could be
more fitting here than Justice, the lady with the scales? Her
eyes are open, and she is therefore able to bring both
balance and peace to the affairs of men.

Scorpio, the Scorpion . . . Judgment, No. XX
   Scorpio is a water sign and hence deals with the emotions. It is said to concern both death and regeneration.

Tarot Key 20, sometimes called the Last Judgment, represents the final state of personal consciousness, which has at last risen from the grave of materiality. Those whose coffins float on the sea of the great subconscious as if they were dead are now regenerated by the trumpet blast of final liberation.

Sagittarius, the Archer . . . the Chariot, No.

Sagittarius is a double-bodied fire sign signifying great driving power and leadership. The Sagittarian is the ambassador of New Thought who travels far in the world of ideas.

Capricorn, the Goat . . . the Devil, No. XV

Capricorn is an earth sign patterned after the horns of a goat. It is the symbol of a ruler, a militarist, a manager—all of them practical and able to function in the material world. Capricorn, the most earthy of the earth triplicity, indicates a person who can be voluntarily enslaved not only by material pleasures and sex but also by science and scientific methods. In Key 15, the Devil wears the goat horns and has been put up on a pedestal by the men and women who, through ignorance and greed, have made themselves the slaves of that which was supposed to serve them.

Aquarius, the Waterman . . . the Star, No. X

The symbol for Aquarius represents the waves made when water is poured from the Waterman's urn. It is an air sign and therefore mental. With impersonal love and altruism, Aquarius gives to all humanity and deals with their problems. Key 17, the Star, is a card of meditation, a mental occupation, the mind reaching out to grasp the solution to problems. Aquarians are said to be intuitive, fond of occult research, and of a naturally meditative turn of mind.

Pisces, the Fishes . . . the Moon, No. XVIII

Pisces is a water sign linked with the emotions; its symbol is composed of two fishes arranged parallel to each other but facing in different directions, or of two crescent moons placed back to back and held together by a band in the middle, representing man's finite consciousness linked to the infinite cosmic consciousness. Man never frees himself from the primitive, emotional side of his nature, though at times he can control it. In Key 18, the Moon, we have many symbols of the evolution of man from the primitive and the path he must follow. Pisces is the most psychic of astrological symbols, and the Moon the most psychic of the Tarot cards; their meanings blend in suggesting a pathway full of temptations as man travels upward on the long journey.

The Spring Equinox has recently moved out of Pisces and into the sign of Aquarius. Before Pisces, it was in the sign of Aries, and before that in Taurus. In Taurus, the bull was worshiped (or the calf), and still is in Spain, where the ritual bullfight retains a symbolism thousands of years old. When Moses railed at his people for worshiping the golden calf, it indicated not only that he did not want them to bow down to idols but also that the Taurian Age was over and that Aries with its ram was the new dispensation. The Piscean Age arrived at about the time of Jesus, and its symbol, the fish, was used extensively in Christian symbology. Now we are moving into the Aquarian Age, and there is the usual confusion in thought and worship that occurs during transitions.

The Christian religion, as we have known it, is felt by many to be losing vitality, and the new Aquarian religion has not yet been revealed. Many have predicted a new savior who has already been born in the East and who will lead us into a universal religion that all present faiths can join in proclaiming. The Tarot and Astrology both show the necessity of combining and balancing force and form, and their followers will probably be among the first to recognize and follow the religion of the dawning Aquarian Age.

EPILOGUE
—THE FOOL'S JOURNEY

The fool is probably the most important card in the entire Tarot deck. Though he may be depicted as a court jester in some packs, in the deck we use in this book A. E. Waite had the card redrawn to match its inner meaning. Waite said of the Fool, in part:

> He is a prince of the other world on his travels through this one—all amidst the morning glory, in the keen air. The sun, which shines behind him, knows whence he came, whither he is going, and how he will return by another path after many days. He is the spirit in each of experience.
>
> Court de Gébelin places it at the head of the whole series as the zero or negative which is presupposed by numeration, and as this is a simpler so also is it a better arrangement. It has been abandoned because in later times the cards have been attributed to the letters of the Hebrew alphabet, and there has been apparently some difficulty about allocating the zero symbol satisfactorily in a sequence of letters all of which signify numbers. . . . The truth is that the real arrangement of the cards has never transpired.

Waite, in his book *The Pictorial Key to the Tarot*, places the Fool between Key 20 and Key 21. We have placed the

Fool as No. 0, before Key 1, for it seems to us that the Fool represents the soul of everyman, which, after it is clothed in a body, appears on earth and goes through the life experiences depicted in the 21 cards of the Major Arcana, sometimes thought of as archetypes of the subconscious.

Let each reader use his imagination and find here his own map of the soul's quest, for these are symbols that are deep within each one of us.

In the Magician and the High Priestess, the Fool learns the uses of the conscious and subconscious aspects of the mind in order to create the bounty of Nature, as pictured in the Empress. The Emperor indicates the role of the ruler, and the Hierophant shows the place of the head of a religious body. In the Lovers, he learns that in order to have a harmonious life, the superconscious must be consulted through the subconscious.

Using his mentality and will, the Fool can ride the Chariot of success as long as he can be master of his passions. The woman in Key 8, Strength, shows him how, through the use of spiritual strength, he can control not only the animal world around him but also the lower forces in himself. The Hermit, with his lantern of Truth, offers to guide him on the spiritual path. When the Fool reaches the Wheel of Fortune, his apprenticeship is over. From now on he is on his own, to rise or fall, while the sphinx of his soul looks on. In Justice, he learns to have a balanced personality and to eliminate the outworn and useless.

He is the Hanged Man who has surrendered himself to Spirit and sacrificed his small desires for the greater one. Key 13 shows him that Death can also be a form of renewal and is not to be feared. The Archangel Michael shows him how to create by pouring the Waters of Life from the unseen into the seen. He has been shown all the secrets of life and how to use them, yet is tempted by the Devil in Key 15 to use his newfound power to create a life of selfish gain and material pleasure.

The Fool is knocked from his material tower and awakened by a flash of spiritual insight to the knowledge that he is on earth to learn and put to use the eternal knowledge he has been given. Chastened, he now learns to meditate, and discovers that no destruction is final. But again, in the Moon card, the Fool is tempted, this time to use his psychic powers for personal glory, and he finds the upward path not only crooked but full of pitfalls. Finally, in the Sun, Key 19, he has learned his lessons well and they have become automatic. He rides forth in control of the horse of the physical— naked, for he no longer has anything to hide. The red feather in his hair shows he now has authority over the animal kingdom, and the sunflowers turning toward him are an indication that all nature turns to the developed soul for future growth.

Next he joins the angel Gabriel in calling all men to awaken to the glories of the spiritual life—and then his journey is over. The Fool is Spirit again, as in the beginning, but now he has passed through his initiations on the material plane, where he has played many parts and learned to control both involution and evolution as he dances the Dance of Life in the very center of the Universe.

GLOSSARY OF
SYMBOLIC TERMS

ANGEL—1. *Raphael*, angel of air. Symbol of the superconscious (Key 6)
  2. *Michael*, angel of fire and sun (Key 14)
  3. *Gabriel*, angel of water (Key 20)

ANKH—Egyptian symbol of life, generation; combines the masculine and feminine (Key 4)

ANUBIS—Jackal-headed Egyptian god representing the evolution of consciousness from lower to higher levels. Also the Egyptian equivalent of Hermes or Mercury, signifying self-consciousness, intellectuality (Key 10)

BANNER (Also STANDARD or FLAG)—Betokens freedom from material bonds; action, vibration. Carried in the left hand, it indicates that control of vibration has passed from the right hand (self-consciousness) to the left (subconsciousness) and has become automatic. (Keys 10, 13, 19, 20)

BULL—Sign of Taurus in Astrology. Assigned to the suit of Pentacles to indicate they are of the element earth

BUTTERFLY—Symbol of the immortality of the soul and of the element air. Knight, Queen, and King of Swords show butterflies in the designs of their cards.

CAT—A black cat indicates the sinister aspect of Venus.

CHAIN—Restriction, largely self-imposed

CIRCLE—Eternity, spirit

CRESCENT—Soul

CROSS—Solar cross has equal arms to indicate the union of the male, positive element (upright), with the female, negative element (horizontal), or the union with God and earth. (Keys 2, 20)

231

CROWN—Attainment, mastery. The Will, which may be set against the cosmic purpose. Represents the creative, formative, and material world. (Keys 3, 5, 16)

CUBE—Sometimes a square. Represents earth, material manifestation. Order and measurement. That which was, is, and shall be. (Key 15)

CUPS—Associated with the concept of water (see suit of Cups, Minor Arcana). The cup is a symbol of knowledge and preservation. It also means love, pleasure, and enjoyment. (Key 14)

CYPRESS TREE—Sacred to Venus (Key 3 and Court cards of Swords)

DEVIL—Symbolizes the false conception that man is bound by material conditions, that he is a slave to necessity and blind chance. The Devil is sensation divorced from understanding by spiritual blindness. (Key 15)

DOG—Friend, helper, and companion to man. Indicates that all nonhuman forms of life are elevated and improved by the advance of human consciousness. (Keys 0, 18)

DOVE—Descent of Spirit, peace

EAGLE—One of the symbols denoting the four seasons or the four suits of the Minor Arcana. The Eagle is associated with Scorpio (the Scorpion), the eighth sign of the Zodiac. It is a symbol of power. (Keys 10, 21)

EARTH—Symbol of concrete physical manifestation (Keys 14, 17)

ELLIPSE—The superconscious (Key 21)

FIGURE EIGHT ON ITS SIDE—Eternal life, the cosmic lemniscate. Harmonious interaction between the conscious and the subconscious, between life and feeling, desire and emotion. May mean dominion over the material. (Keys 1, 8)

FISH—Idea or thought. In the King of Cups the fish is seen coming from the sea of the universal subconscious. In Page of Cups it is arising from his own subconscious.

FLAME—Spirit

FLOWERS—White flowers: spiritual thoughts, love, happiness. Red flowers: human desires

FRUIT—Fertility

GLOBE—(See Orb of the World.) Symbol of dominion (Key 4)

GNOMES—Elementals who live beneath the surface of the earth. Associated with the suit of Pentacles.

GOAT—Fertility, as when depicted on the arms of the throne of the Queen of Pentacles. Suggests bestiality and over-indulgence in sex, as in Key 15, the Devil.

GOLD—Metal of the sun

GRAPES—Abundance, pleasure. GRAPEVINES; a continuation and growth in abundance and pleasure

HAND—Right hand, positive, masculine; left hand, negative, feminine

HEART—Symbols in the shape of a heart refer to the sub-conscious, the emotions. (Key 3)

HORSE—Symbol of solar energy, or the controlled, subdued Life-force. (Keys 13, 19)

IHVH—Ancient Hebrew initials of the name Jehovah: I—Fire; H—Water; V—Air; H—Earth (Key 10)

IRIS—Represents Iris, Greek goddess of the rainbow, as in Key 14

KEYS CROSSED—The Hidden Doctrine. One is a silver, the other gold—representing solar and lunar currents in radiant energy. (Key 5)

LAMP—Spiritual light, intelligence

LEAVES—Growth, vitality

LIGHT—Spiritual emanations, activity of God, life

LIGHTNING—A flash of inspiration. The Life-power that descends down the Kabalistic Tree of Life

LILY—Abstract thought untinged by desire (Key 1)

LION—King of the beasts; zodiacal sign Leo. Represents all-powerful subhuman force. May also stand for Mars (war). (Keys 8, 10, 21)

MIRROR OF VENUS—A solar cross surmounted by a circle; symbol of the planet Venus; idicates fertility (Key 4)

MOON—A feminine astrological symbol of personality, also of the subconscious mind. The reflected light of the subconscious (Keys 2, 18)

MOUNTAINS (SNOW-CAPPED PEAKS)—Indicate the cold, abstract principles of mathematics behind and above all warm, colorful, and vital activities of cosmic manifestation. Heights of abstract thought. Wisdom and understanding (Keys 0, 6, 14, 20)

ORB OF THE WORLD—A traditional symbol of the earth dominated by the Lord or the Spirit. (Key 4)

PALM—Symbol of victory over death, and of the male aspect
of life. The active force, as shown on the veil behind
the High Priestess. (Key 2)

PATH—The way to spiritual attainment and esoteric knowledge, as set forth in the Tarot cards (Keys 14, 18)

PENTACLE—The pentagram in the form of an amulet, believed to protect against evil spirits (See suit of Pentacles, also Key 15.)

PENTAGRAM (SEAL OF SOLOMON)—Five-pointed star, ex-
pressing mind's domination over the elements. Symbol
of the Word made Flesh. Depending on the direction
of its points, it may represent order or confusion. (Note
that the pentagrams are right side up in the suit of
Pentacles, reversed in Key 15.)

PILLAR—1. *White Pillar* (Jachin) establishes the principle
    inherent in all things; the positive aspect of life;
    light

    2. *Black Pillar* (Boaz). Negation of activity, in-
    ertia; darkness (Keys 2, 5, 11)

POMEGRANATES—Symbol of the female, passive aspect of
life; fecundity (Key 2)

PYRAMID—The earth in its maternal aspect. The triangular-
shaped face of the pyramid suggests the threefold
principle of creation.

RABBIT—Symbol of fertility

RAINBOW—A Sign from God of future protection and happiness

RAM'S HEAD—Symbol of Mars, war; power, leadership. Also
First Sign of the Zodiac (Aries, the Ram) (Key 4)

ROSE—1. *White Rose*: Freedom from lower forms of desire
    and passion

    2. *Red Rose*: represents Venus, nature, desire
    Both are cultivated flowers, representing cultural
    activities. (Keys 0, 1)

SALAMANDER—Lizardlike creature able to live in the midst
of fire. The elemental of the suit of Wands; also used
in the Court cards

SCALES—Balanced judgment (Key 11)

SCROLL—The Divine Law, the Hidden Mysteries. Past events
impressed upon the subconscious (Key 2)

SERPENT—Symbol of wisdom, for it tempts man to knowledge of himself. Secrecy, subtlety. Serpent biting its tail

represents law of endless transformation; also represents radiant energy descending into manifestation. (Keys 1, 6, 10)

SHELLFISH—The early stages of conscious unfoldment. Related to the Zodiacal Sign of the Crab. May invade the territory of the waking consciousness and give rise to fears. (Key 18)

SHIP—Material treasure

SILVER—Metal of the moon

SPHINX—Symbol of the combination of human and animal attributes. The white sphinx betokens mercy; the black one, severity. Sometimes the Sphinx represents the human senses, which are continually propounding riddles. (Keys 7, 10)

SQUARE—Foursquare, the solidity of earth

STAFF—Implement of the Magician; emblem of power

STAR—Suggests Sixth Sign of the Zodiac. The six-pointed star (hexagram) indicates dominion over laws of the great world; the eight-pointed star represents cosmic order, radiant energy. (Keys 9, 17)

STONE—*Abn* is the Hebrew word for stone. *Aba*, stemming from the first two letters of the alphabet, means "father" (as in ABraham); *Bn* means "son" (*cf.* Ben-Gurion, son of Gurion). Thus, stone symbolizes the union of father and son, spirit and body; the Divine Wisdom and the human intellect. "Upon this rock [stone] will I build my church" (on the understanding that the Father and the Son are one). David slew Goliath with a stone, and with this understanding we can all slay the Goliaths in our lives.

STREAM—Symbolizes the stuff of life, forever flowing to the ocean of cosmic consciousness.

SUN—Source of light, dynamo of radiant energy whence all creatures derive their personal force (Keys 0, 6, 13, 19)

SUNFLOWERS—Nature in its fullness (Key 19)

SWORDS—Represent activity, either destructive or constructive (*see* suit of Swords). They also represent the rigors of the law; can mean the elimination of outworn forms. (Key 11)

SYLPH—An elemental of the air somewhat similar to a cupid. Associated with the suit of Swords

TOWER—Represents a man's creation or personality, sometimes built on a foundation of false science. Misappre-
hension; the fallacy of personal isolation (Keys 13,
16, 18)

TREE—1. *Tree of Knowledge of Good and Evil*, bearing five
fruits, representing the five senses (in Key 6, it is
seen behind Eve).

     2. *Tree of Life*, bearing 12 fruits, representing the
12 signs of the Zodiac (Key 6, behind Adam).
Note: Under the appellations of the Tree of Life
and the Tree of the Knowledge of Good and Evil
is concealed the great arcanum of antiquity—the
mystery of equilibrium. The Tree of Life represents the spiritual point of balance—the secret of
immortality. The Tree of the Knowledge of Good
and Evil represents polarity or imbalance—the
secret of mortality. Though humanity is still
wandering in the world of good and evil, it will
ultimately attain completion and eat of the fruit
of the Tree of Life growing in the midst of the
illusionary garden of worldly things

UNDINE—An elemental that lives in the water and is thus
associated with the suit of Cups. Undines appear on
the throne of the Queen of Cups.

VEIL—Indicates hidden things or ideas. Symbol of virginity.
Only when the veil is rent or penetrated by concentrated impulses on self-conscious levels are the
creative activities of the subconscious realized and
actualized. (Keys 2, 11)

WAND—Symbol of Will and power. Suggests continual renewal of life. May have phallic significance. (*See* suit
of Wands, also Key 21.)

WATER—Symbolizes the subconscious, the emotions. Water
in a pool symbolizes the reservoir of cosmic mind stuff,
which can be stirred into vibration by the act of meditation. (Keys 14, 17, 18, 20)

WATER LILIES—Eternal life

WHEAT—Abundance and fertility. Sacred to Hathor-Isis and
all Mother goddesses. (Key 3)

WHEEL—Symbol of the whole cycle of cosmic expression.
The center or pivot is the archetypal or thought world;
the inner circle, creative; middle circle, formative; and

the outer circle, the material world. The eight spokes, like the eight-pointed star, represent the channels of universal radiant energy. (Keys 7, 10)

WOLF—Symbolizes the manifestations of Nature before man has tamed and civilized them. (Key 18)

WREATH—Represents the forces of Nature, the kingdom of growing things. (Keys 3, 8, 21)

YOD (DROPS OF LIGHT)—Yod is the Hebrew letter symbolizing the hands of man. It betokens power, skill, dexterity. The descent of the Life-force from above into the conditions of material existence. Corresponds to the zodiacal sign of the Virgin. (Keys 16, 18)

ZERO—Symbol of the absence of quality, quantity, and mass. Denotes absolute freedom from every limitation. Sign of the infinite and eternal conscious energy. Superconsciousness (Key 0)

ZODIAC—Symbol of cycle of existence

BIBLIOGRAPHY

BENJAMINE, ELBERT (C. C. Zain): *Sacred Tarot.*
Los Angeles: Church of Light, 1935.

CASE, PAUL FOSTER: *The Tarot.*
New York: Macoy Publishing Co., 1947.

CROWLEY, ALEISTER: *777 Revisited.*
London: Neptune Press, 1955.

CURTISS, HARRIETTE, and HOMER, F.: *The Key of Destiny.*
San Francisco: Curtiss Philosophic Book Co., 1923.

FORTUNE, DION: *The Mystical Qabalah.*
London: Williams & Margate, Ltd., 1938.

FRATER, S.M.R.D., and others: *Book "T"—The Tarot.*
Gloucester, England: Helios, 1967.

GRAY, EDEN: *Recognition—Themes on Inner Perception.*
Stroudsburg, Pa.: Inspiration House Publications, 1969.
———: *The Tarot Revealed.*
New York: Bell Publishing Co. (Crown), 1969.

GRAY, WILLIAM G.: *The Ladder of Lights.*
Toddington: Helios Book Service, Ltd., 1968.

INSIGHT INSTITUTE: *How to Read the Tarot* (study course).
Worcester Park, England.

KNIGHT, GARETH: *A Practical Guide to Qabalistic Symbolism* (Vols. 1 and 2).
Toddington: Helios Book Service, Ltd., 1965.

LIND, FRANK: *How to Understand the Tarot.*
London: Bazaar, Exchange and Mart, Ltd.

MATHERS, S. L. MACGREGOR: *The Tarot* (pamphlet).
New York: Occult Research Press.

MAYANANDA: *The Tarot for Today.*
London: Zeus Press, 1963.

PAPUS: *The Tarot of the Bohemians.*
New York: Arcanum Books, 1958.

239

Pushong, Carlyle A.: *The Tarot of the Magi.*
  London and New York: Regency Press, 1969.
Rakoczi, Basil Ivan: *The Painted Caravan.*
  The Hague: L. J. C. Boucher, 1954.
Waite, Arthur Edward: *The Pictorial Key to the Tarot.*
  Wm. Rider & Son, Ltd.: London, 1922.
Westcott, William Wynn: *The Study of the Kabalah.*
  New York: Allied Publications.
————: *The Sepher Yetzirah* (translation). Pamphlet.
  New York: Occult Research Press.

Index

ABOUT THE AUTHOR

A former actress who has appeared with Katharine Cornell, Frederic March, and Brian Aherne, Miss Eden Gray has traveled all over the world. She was leading woman in a play in London and helped to produce several plays for the London theater.

For ten years, Miss Gray owned a bookstore-publishing house in New York City and published a number of books on metaphysical themes. She has given classes in how to read the Tarot cards in New York and in Palm Beach, and has lectured and taught classes in Science of Mind at the First Church of Religious Science in New York and a number of other cities. For three years she has had her own radio program and now continues her work as a writer and practitioner at her home in Pennsylvania.

OTHER WORLDS.
OTHER REALITIES.

In fact and fiction, these extraordinary books bring the fascinating world of the supernatural down to earth. From ancient astronauts and black magic to witchcraft, voodoo and mysticism——these books look at other worlds and examine other realities.

☐ **CHARIOTS OF THE GODS** (Q5753/$1.25)—Fact
☐ **THE EXORCIST** (X7200/$1.75)—Fiction
☐ **WITCHCRAFT AND BLACK MAGIC** (R6836/$1.45)—Fact
☐ **RAGA SIX** (Q7249/$1.25)—Fiction
☐ **POWER THROUGH WITCHCRAFT** (N5713/95¢)—Fact
☐ **HELL HOUSE** (N7277/95¢)—Fiction
☐ **I CHING** (Q5214/$1.25)—Fact
☐ **A COMPLETE GUIDE TO THE TAROT** (Q6696/$1.25)—Fact
☐ **GODS FROM OUTER SPACE** (Q7276/$1.25)—Fact